Quench The Lamp

QUENCH THE LAMP

Alice Taylor

BRANDON

First published in 1990 by
Brandon Book Publishers Ltd
Dingle, Co. Kerry, Ireland

British Library Cataloguing in Publication Data
Taylor, Alice
    Quench the lamp.
    1. Ireland (Republic). Social life, 1949-
    —Biographies
    I. Title
    941.70823092

    ISBN 0-86322-112-2

1 2 3 4 5 6 7 8 9 10

Cover design: Paula Nolan
Printed by Richard Clay Ltd, Bungay, Suffolk

To my mother, who lit a candle in all our hearts

Contents

Children Of A Changing Time

THIS IS THE story of country living that revolved around the hearth, the family, the farm animals, and the neighbours. The people we lived amongst provided us with companionship, whether out in the fields or around the fire, and the farmyard and household chores gave a pattern to our days. But as we left childhood behind and put tentative toes into the adult world, that pattern changed; rural living moved forward into a bright new world and we became the last children of the old ways.

So this is also the story of a changing time, a time when rural Ireland quenched the oil lamp, removed the po from under the bed and threw the black pots and iron kettles under the hedge. We who were the children of the forties came in the fifties into the challenging, exciting world of adolescence.

Rural electrification flooded our homes with light, clearing away old ghosts and beliefs and sending fairies scurrying underground. Modern plumbing replaced the bucket of spring water from the well and the timber rain-barrel at the gable end.

Corners hitherto shrouded in dust and tranquility suddenly found themselves scrubbed clinically clean with the new and plentiful supply of hot water and disinfectant. The flush toilet replaced the chamber-pot, bringing an instant solution to a basic problem. The wide, warm comforting arms of the open fire were folded up and into its corner came tight-lipped ranges and shining enamel-faced cookers.

Out in the farm the clip-clop of horses' hooves gave way to the roar of engines; cows, accustomed to the soft glow of the storm-lantern as we checked them at night, now blinked in the glare of the harsh electric light.

The older generation stood and hesitated on the brink of this bright new world, but we of a younger generation opened wide our arms and swam happily with the tide. We became the young parents of the sixties and seventies and brought children into a world totally different from the one of our own childhoods. Economic prosperity boomed and our teenagers grew up far from the shadows cast by the oil lamp and the plaintive call of the corncrake.

Look back with me to when we changed from the old ways to the new and left behind a world now almost forgotten.

Going For
The Messages

I ALWAYS STOPPED for a few seconds outside Ned's door to sniff the air appreciatively as we walked up the winding street past his little shop on our way to Mass. The whiff of tea, loose in a plywood chest; a wheel of cheese wrapped in a muslin cloth; candles piled on top of each other in a timber box: all mixed with the strong smell of snuff, which he kept in a tall tin can under the counter. He cut plugs of tobacco off a large block, filling the little shop with rich aromas which blended with the other fragrances that made up the unique mixture that was Ned's shop.

Ned was a little man clad in a brown overall and because he seldom came out from behind his high timber counter he created a head and shoulders image in our minds. His hair had receded well back from his forehead but had decided then to go no further. His hair-line was a blend of grey and brown, matching his brown overall which was streaked with white as a result of his constant weighing of flour. He viewed the world with kind, brown eyes from behind steel-rimmed spectacles.

Although his working hours often extended far into the night he was always, it seemed, in a pleasant frame of mind and when he was not serving customers he was busy weighing out supplies into stiff, brown paper bags. Goods were delivered in large jute sacks and heavy timber boxes and had to be measured out into weights suitable for purchase by his customers. Tea, sugar and flour were all poured into these strong brown bags with different sized scoops. They were then thumped gently on the counter to settle down the contents before being put back on the old iron scales for the final test of precise weight. The balancing weights ranged from small round brass ounces to heavy oblong iron pounds which had holding bars for convenience. Ned had a white enamel scales as well, but this was for the weighing of lighter items which called for greater precision, like cheese, tobacco and sweets. The long needle waved back and forth like the hand of a clock gone crazy until finally it settled and pointed out the exact weight.

On the floor inside the counter Ned stood surrounded by a circle of bags of varying heights. He usually began Monday morning with flour weighing and as the day progressed the shelf behind him filled up with paper bags of different sizes while the white cotton bag of flour declined in stature. The jute sack of sugar was next on the agenda and Ned weighed away, in between patiently serving and chatting to customers as they came and went, and after that he started on the tea. His appearance always told the tale of exactly what he had been weighing because evidence of it clung to his overall.

High on the shelves behind him, flash lamps, bicycle repair kits, Sacred Heart lamps, alarm clocks and all sorts of things stood. Below them were tins of biscuits that had to be weighed out when customers made their choices. Some containers had glass tops so that you could peer in without Ned having to remove the covers, and below the biscuits came the tin gallons and high glass jars of sweets whose colourful contents provided temptation beyond resistance. There were black-and-white bull's-eyes which were hard enough to damage the most perfect teeth and "brown cushions" with their strange, minty taste; but the conversation lozenges made for the brightest jar of all, with their gay pinks, reds and yellows. They were exactly as their name implied, but the conversation was not one to be had with a casual acquaintance, as the messages had a decidedly intimate flavour. "Kiss me quick" or "Love me" or "Hug me" were not invitations to be extended to all and sundry. As if to counteract these amorous sweets came the acid drops that made you catch your breath with their sharp tang. Gallon sweets were the poor relations; the grander ones came in the glass jars. Top of the market came the sweets that had their own coats on, the wrapped variety. We seldom rose to those heady heights but the plain-wrapped toffees at six for a penny came within our reach. For long-lasting sucking the slab of hard toffee was the best value and came with the titles "Captain Mac" and "Half-Time Jimmy"; the full slab was usually beyond our means, so Ned cracked off the required amount on the edge of the counter.

Everything that Ned had to handle was inside the counter, while outside was anything that did not require weighing or wrapping. A stack of enamel and tin buckets stood guard on each side of a pile of enamel pots and pans. Spades, shovels, two-prong and four-prong pikes and pickaxes all stood shoulder to shoulder, while milking stools could be tested for balance and comfort by waiting customers or anyone stopping in for a chat. Hanging off the ceiling was a miscellaneous assortment of goods, including kettles and teapots, balls of binder twine, strong nailed boots, and occasionally a pig's head. You had to keep your eye on the pig's head as sometimes if you stood underneath it you could get a cold drip of salty brine on top of your head. If you looked up, the pig's eye would peer contemptuously down at you. On Friday the pig's head gave way to strips of salted ling that hung off the ceiling like items of forgotten underwear.

13

Window-dressing was not Ned's speciality: out there stood sun-faded advertising placards of teas being sampled by rosy-cheeked ladies and foggy mirrors etched with happy, pot-bellied, bearded gentlemen advocating the bliss of St Bruno tobacco. Ned's cat used these mirrors to admire her tawney good looks and to improve on them. The window was the cat's department and from here she watched life pass by with the disdainful air that only a well-bred cat can impart, her unblinking stare occasionally punctuated by the flick of an aristocratic feline whisker. A sliding timber shutter, which no longer slid but reluctantly shunted, gave access to this view of the outside world.

Ned's burning passions in life were horses and greyhounds and his "mother bitch", as he called his oldest greyhound, was usually to be seen stretched out on the shop floor between the buckets and shovels. She knew all Ned's customers and if a stranger called, which was rare enough, she slowly drew herself off her haunches and sniffed him out, much to the customer's surprise, because a sniffer dog was something one did not expect to find in this little corner of the world. But the greyhound, like Ned himself, was not aggressive, merely curious.

Ned used the evenings to do his accounts, which meant adding up the totals in a stack of little notebooks. Each of his customers had a notebook into which they wrote their messages, and these they handed in to Ned together with their shopping bags. Many farmers called to him for their messages on the way home from the creamery and scarcely needed to write down their orders since he knew better than they did what they needed. He filled each bag and wrote the prices into each notebook, and once a week or twice a month, whichever the arrangement was, he added up the list and was paid.

GOING FOR THE MESSAGES

When he had his accounts finished he folded his arms on the counter-top and became the ideal chairman who skilfully directed heated arguments into calm waters and often supervised the sale of greyhound pups and promising yearlings. The shop, as well as being a place for trading, was also a select men's club where male views were aired and membership was based on a man's knowledge of horses and dogs. Not that anyone was refused entry, but as the main topics of conversation were racing odds and filly fitness, unless you were that way inclined you could not take part in the discussions that went on late into the night. Men sat around on milking stools, upturned buckets, tea-chests and indeed sometimes on an upturned po and, as the talk flowed, the smoke from their pipes and cigarettes curled upwards, blending with the pigs' heads and balls of binder twine, giving them a smoky, well-seasoned look. Speedy greyhounds such as Spanish Battleship and Prince of Bermuda were discussed, their finer points closely analysed, and the chances of local horses Sheila's Cottage and Cottage Rake winning the big races were argued back and forth at length.

The only night that Ned had early closing was when the track was on, but that did not upset his regulars as they were all at the greyhound track as well. He closed down completely for Listowel and Galway races, and sometimes for other meetings if a horse of special interest happened to be running. No one else could follow the geography of Ned's shop, so the simple solution was to shut down altogether. Everybody understood that when Ned's door was closed he had gone racing. Perishable goods he sold off to his old pals the night before and it was not unusual to see a man walking home from Ned's with a pig's head under his arm.

My mother brought the messages from town every Sunday after Mass but sometimes during the week one of us might be sent in to bring home extra requirements. We loved to be sent to town so there was great competition to be the one chosen to go. Walking along the road I enjoyed looking in through the iron gates on my way and watching the animals in the different fields, or climbing to the top of the ditch and looking down over the valley. Arriving in town I went straight to Ned's shop, where I was always sure of a fistful of sweets; he made no profit out of me and I had it eaten before I left the shop. Children and men were Ned's best customers because some of the less understanding women felt that in the interests of hygiene his cat should be evicted from her viewing perch in the window.

Across the road from Ned lived two old ladies, the Miss Bowlers, who had a big stone-floored shop that was scrubbed out daily. It was a contrast to Ned's, where the timber floorboards, ingrained with knots and seams, sank and squeaked as you clattered across them. Whereas Ned's little shop was packed to overflowing, the Miss Bowlers' large shop had all the activity packed into one corner where they dished out squares of home-made toffee, sold brown lemonade and cut up blocks of ice-cream and sandwiched it between two wafers. A penny ice-cream only served to stimulate the taste-buds, a twopenny one was more satisfying and a fourpenny one bordered on extravagance, while a sixpenny one was sheer, gorgeous gluttony. They also sold puffy buns with dollops of cream and jam inside; when you sank your teeth into them the cream oozed around the corners of your mouth and along your fingers and, like Ned's cat, you had to whip your tongue around vigorously lest you lose any luscious lick.

One of the sisters was like the cream-buns she sold and had folds of soft double chins, beneath which rows of white pearls continued the cascading descent into her enormous cleavage. Her hair was snow-white, and even though it was caught up at the back it still curled down over her forehead and ears, from which long pearl earrings swung, while her large, soft bosom encased in a white, satin blouse rested on the counter-top. She always reminded me of a downy feather pillow, soft, white and comfortable. The other sister paled by comparison. She was tall, thin and spare and was like the tall bottles of lemonade whose tops she whipped off with the iron bottle opener.

What Ned lacked in fastidiousness the Miss Bowlers made up for: their shop and they themselves were spotless. The hands of the small, cuddly Miss Bowler were white and soft, with pale pink fingernails which curved to slight points, and she always smelt like a rose garden, waves of light, flowery perfume wafting from beneath flowing folds. The tall sister seemed clinically clean and wore a white, lace collar and cuffs over her long black dress; her auburn hair streaked with grey stayed in a tight knot at the base of her poll where it was secured firmly with a few barbaric-looking hairpins.

As well as serving us ice-cream, buns and lemonade, they taught us manners in a very gentle fashion. So restraining was their influence that once you stepped inside their shop-door you slowed down to a ladylike pace and approached their counter with a sense of decorum, stating your requirements in a clear, precise voice and never omitting "please" and "thank you". The Miss Bowlers dealt only in the luxuries of life and graced each transaction with such a sense of occasion that you felt they lived in a special world and you were their welcome guest rather than a child with a few pence in your fist.

Around the corner from the Miss Bowlers was Con the baker who every day turned out rows of high-backed crusty loaves on his low timber counter while the smell from his little bakery behind the shop spilled out into

17

the street and signalled that another batch was fresh
out of the oven. Big currant-buns with sticky white icing
pouring down their sides clung together at the base, and
if you wanted one Con eased them apart, but if you were
lucky enough to be buying more they came in a row with
the currants protruding through the icing like stones on
a snow-covered hill. He made huge bracks and seed
loaves that were only bought if you were expecting
visitors or having the Stations, or if Christmas was
around the corner. But his hot, golden doughnuts,
oozing warm, syrupy sugar, that melted in your mouth
and slid down your throat like butter in a warm dish
were the best of all. Tuesday and Thursday were dough-
nut days and their smell transcended all others, enfold-
ing us in delightful waves of anticipation before we ever
sank our yearning teeth into their steamy sweetness.

All our clothes, or the material for making them,
were bought in the one shop. Here my mother could buy
elastic for our knickers or material to make an overcoat
for my father. Here, indeed, she could buy cover of all
kinds for bodies of all shapes and sizes, from inside out
and from top to toe. Long rolls of material stretched out
on the high shelves and when Jack unrolled it in great
thumps it fell into billowing folds on top of the long
timber counter. Catching up fistfuls of it and shaking it
like a dog might shake a rabbit, he would say, "Look at
that for quality".

He had a fascinating practice, which he shared with
my mother, of catching a little bit of the material
between thumb and index finger of both hands and
giving it a few hard, fast pulls which caused the cloth,
if it was heavy, to give a dull thud or, if lighter, a hard,
sharper sound. This was known as testing the bias. A lot
of discussion went into assessing the quality of the
weave and testing the bias. Buying material was not
something to be treated lightly and often the decision

would be stretched over a few Sundays before all were
satisfied that a particular cloth was the right one to see
father through the next ten winters or to provide a
daughter with a Sunday coat which would have the
handing down potential to serve a couple of younger
ones in succeeding years. Purchasing the material was
only the first step in this process. The next necessitated
a visit to the tailor or dressmaker, and would inevitably
be followed by several further visits for fitting at later
stages. And because the full creation of an outfit was a
long-drawn-out process, it was of the greatest importance to make sure that the first step was the right one.
All in all, such purchases could not be concluded in a
hurry and Jack, fortunately, had all the time and
patience in the world to devote to discussing the pros
and cons of pure wool versus velour or tweed. When the
material had finally been decided upon he measured it
along the brass rule on the counter.

Jack had big boxes of shirts and stockings and endless varieties of underwear. Heating everywhere was of
a limited nature and layers of underwear provided vital
protection against the cold. My mother fought valiantly
to force us into a scaled-down version of long johns
called combinations, and their name was very apt
because they combined total cover from wrist to knee
with a built-in back door providing the necessary outlet.
They were hideous and uncomfortable and we refused,
point blank, to be fettered by them. My mother believed
that if you were warm, all other considerations were
secondary and such thinking led to many protestations
from her five daughters; sometimes she got the better of
us, but not where the combinations were concerned.

Our footwear, too, was bought at Jack's. He lifted us
easily onto the counter and marched us up and down to
ensure a good fit. A fine, tall man of ample proportions,
he was always well turned out, as befitted his business,

19

in a grey or navy suit with matching waistcoat and a
gold watch-chain draped across his broad chest. Completely bald, his face and head knew no boundaries and
his skin had a pale, polished look, in contrast to the
brown, weatherbeaten appearance of his customers.
His spectacles, when not in use, he wore perched on top
of his head, a feat that I greatly admired.

Paying Jack was a seasonal event, depending on
many things: a good milk cheque, the sale of fattened
pigs, or a good harvest. When the farmers did well, Jack
did well. He recorded all transactions in a big leather-
bound ledger which he kept on a little rostrum inside
the window.

Only rarely did we visit the harness-maker as my
father repaired most of the tackling himself. A tall,
rangy man, he doled out good advice as well as leather
work. Once, when my father and he were discussing the
women in their lives and the reasons why sometimes
they were a bit touchy, Billy's prescription was: "Let the
women out to take the edge off them". Housebound
women, he figured, were cranky women. Billy himself
was not endowed with a great amount of patience. Big-
hearted, colourful and generous he certainly was, but
he was not easily amused. Many years after I had left
childhood behind me I went home to the funeral of an old
man who was also noted for being particularly serious
by nature.

"Taylor," he said (he called us all Taylor because he
never knew which of us girls he was talking to), "how
well you came down for old Bob's funeral."

"Well, Billy," I said, "he served us faithfully all his
life."

"Yes," said Billy solemnly, "without a smile on his
face."

What made me relish the remark was the fact that
Billy himself rarely smiled.

GOING FOR THE MESSAGES

The same families had been in most of the shops for several generations and had built up and passed on a deep understanding and knowledge of their customers. It was a relationship that worked both ways, and when money was scarce we gave each other mutual support. While all the shopkeepers were our neighbours, my mother always bore in mind that we were related to some of them, for she was a great believer in looking after the needs of the extended family. Allegiances of all kinds were important to her, and if somebody's grandmother had been good to my mother's grandmother then my mother was not going to forget that, and so all the shopkeepers – Jack, Ned, Con, Billy and the Miss Bowlers – were not just shopkeepers to us: they were our friends, and shopping was as much a social outing as the acquiring of goods.

Mrs Tom's Tan

A T THE AGE of ten I received my first lesson in male treachery. I was naive and trusting at that point of my development and thought that life was a fairy-tale full of happy endings. He was twelve; tall, thin, blond and devastating, the only boy in a family of four girls, the family treasure. Our mothers were cousins and he came from the city to spend one long, hot summer on our farm – his first visit to the country. On his arrival I viewed him with a certain amount of suspicion. Dressed in immaculate white shorts and pullover, he possessed long, brown, unscratched legs. It was the unscratched legs I distrusted most because they must have been acquired by sunbathing on a manicured lawn, an activity that was almost inconceivable as far as I was concerned.

Another possible explanation seemed even more unthinkable. The only time I had seen legs like those was when Tom's wife decided for herself that summer had arrived. Tom was a neighbouring farmer who had emigrated and had then returned home bringing a glamorous English wife with him. We children referred to her only as Tom's wife, which was strange really because she was a colourful person in her own right, but I never learned her own name so we called her Tom's wife or Mrs Tom.

One year, after a long, cold spring, the first sunny

day of summer came and on the way home from school that evening we met Mrs Tom walking along on a pair of positively golden, tanned legs. How was it possible? Legs that had been clad in lyle stockings and which I had assumed to be pale and milky underneath, now were suddenly golden brown. Surrounded as I had always been by all the natural voices of the countryside telling me of seasonal change, I knew that in nature nothing was instant, and so the extraordinary spectacle of Mrs Tom's legs turning brown overnight captured my imagination. It puzzled me for days and then, in order to solve my problem, I eventually went straight to the heart of the matter and asked her to explain the transformation. She looked at me in surprise for a few moments, causing me to think that I had pushed my luck too far, but then she smiled.

"Come with me," she said, "and I'll show you."

Taking me into her bedroom, she picked up a bottle from a bewildering array of pots and jars on her dressing-table and clarified the mystery of her instant tan. And from that day onwards I marked the arrival of summer by the change in the colour of Mrs Tom's legs. The first daffodils heralded the arrival of spring and Mrs Tom's legs announced when summer was here.

My cousin with legs like Mrs Tom's was the cause of great curiosity and my first impulse was to run this paragon of perfection through a *glaise* to discover if the tan would wash off. I also felt that a struggle with a blackthorn hedge would do him no harm and might even make him look more like one of us. However, his mother and sisters stayed for the first few days of his visit and decorum had to be observed while they remained on the scene. During those few days, as if to emphasize the wild state of my own legs, I scratched myself on barbed wire and gained a scar which, though not deep, ran from my knee to my ankle. In ordinary circumstances it would have been left to heal of its own accord but my mother's cousin was a nurse and she insisted on washing the wound with disinfectant and putting a big long strip of sticking plaster on my leg. This made the whole thing look a lot more serious than it really was and I went around explaining to the less well-informed that I could actually have died from blood poisoning.

Robert – for that was my brown-legged cousin's name – was left to fare for himself when his mother and sisters had departed, and he and I teamed up together. I took him catching "collies" and discovered that his tan did not wash off, walked him in his snow-white canvas sandals into his first cow dung, and took him picking blackberries. He worked in the meadow making hay, blistering his hands on the pike handle, and went for spins in the float, tearing a hole in the backside of his pants. People who came to the house gradually stopped asking who was the visitor because he no longer stood out from the crowd.

Sometimes late in the evening we went to the well for water and, sitting down on the side of the mossy hill with high ferns forming an umbrella over our heads, we told each other stories in a cool green fairyland where the evening sun slanted through the serrated fronds of ferns. Walking through the dry gap, we cooled our dusty toes in the ice-cold stream that overflowed from the deep well into the adjacent *glaise*. The stones in that stream were black, flat and smooth and, stacked on top of one another, made a rocker which tested our ability to balance as far forwards and backwards as possible without toppling over. Frogs, too, liked this little corner because it was moist and cool, sheltered by overhanging trees. We rested hands and knees on the large grey stone that fronted the well which arched back into the hill and, leaning forward, we watched our wavering

reflections in its depths. At that time I had a story in my
schoolbook about Narcissus who, looking into a well, fell
in love with his own reflection. I pondered on the im-
probability of this as I watched my long blonde hair
blend with Robert's in the water of the well.

Getting up early in the morning, we went out picking
mushrooms in the clinging, misty dew of the new dawn.
We watched the sauntering cows scattering moisture
along the high grass as they went in for milking, and on
reaching home we grilled our salt-sprinkled mushrooms on a hot sod of turf by the open fire.

Catching collies was our favourite occupation. Late
in the evening we came with our swinging jam-crocks to
the river which curled between high banks over dark
brown stones, sometimes shallow and sandy and then
curving into deep, still pools where trout jumped with a
splash, sending ripples circling to the bank and diffusing the midges which hung suspended over the water.
My dream was to catch a trout in a jam-crock and the
practical impossibility of such an achievement never
dampened my enthusiasm. We splashed around in the
river until daylight moved towards dusk and then we
rambled home in semi-darkness through the fields,
where the cows now rested chewing the cud.

I loved the cows and introduced Robert to them
individually by name. Back in the stalls I showed him
where each one belonged and told him how they all
knew their own places. When he suggested that they
should have place names over their heads I was fascinated by the idea. That each cow would have her own
name over her head was a new and wonderful thought.
Ours were going to be the first cows in the country to
have their names mounted in their executive offices.
But how to achieve such a dream was the question, and
Robert had the answer. Back in the city the railway
station had a machine that could print on tin and he

would do all the cows' names and send them on to me. It seemed a dream come true and I was sure that the cows would be delighted as well. With a stubby pencil and a notebook I laboriously wrote out each cow's name and, for good measure, added the horses as well, in case they might feel neglected.

I was sorry when the time came for Robert to go home, but the thought of the cows' name-plates arriving compensated for any pangs of regret that I might have felt at his departure. I got a jamjar and filled it with short, shiny tacks which I dug out of my father's butter box, doing untold damage to my fingertips and nails. I also helped myself to a small, stubby hammer, which I knew he would go rooting for, but as he could never find anything anyway I felt that one more missing item would not make that much difference.

With everything in readiness for action, I waited for the name-plates to arrive. Every day I watched for the postman and every day I drew a blank but decided, each time, that tomorrow my parcel would surely come. Eventually, after many weeks, I finally gave up hope. I felt betrayed on behalf of my cows, who were to remain apparently nameless, and I told myself that I should not have expected much from a boy who had legs as smooth and perfect as Mrs Tom's tan.

Old Bags

THE ART OF making do was a virtue passed down from my great-aunt Susan through the female line of our family – mere males were not considered to be safe custodians of such gems of wisdom – and practised in our constant saving and re-using of almost everything. Containers of many kinds were used and used again and the only waste-disposal unit we knew was the pigs' trough.

Jamjars were washed and stored carefully for future use for home-made jams and preserves, and any we couldn't use ourselves we returned to the shop for a penny for a two-pound pot and a halfpenny for a one-pound one. As potential sources of pocket-money, few jampots were left lying around for long. Another container with multiple uses was the tin sweet gallon. Having booked a gallon with Ned, we got it after a while with little bits of sweets clinging to the bottom, but we soon cleaned it out and had it ready for its new life. Tea was taken to the meadow in a gallon if the *meitheal* was small or to supplement the white enamel bucket if the workforce was strong, and sometimes a lone man would drink straight from the gallon. It also served to take milk between the houses when supplies were low in the winter time, and for bringing water from the well, especially if you were too small to carry a bucket.

Some farmers kept a goat with their herd of cows,

and people without grazing for cows usually had goats which fed off ditches and were satisfied with limited supplies of grass. The versatile gallon was used for milking the goat, though the milker had to take care not to get more than milk in the gallon – the odd angle from which goats were milked made this a tricky exercise. And the gallon was also one of the many different kinds of containers used for collecting eggs.

The soft brown tissue-paper around the Sunday loaf of bread was folded carefully to be used later for wrapping up our school lunches. Empty bottles of many kinds were rinsed with water and sand and re-employed as lunch bottles. The milk of magnesia bottle gave its contents a blue look; small Paddy whiskey bottles also made the trip to school, but old sauce bottles accompanied us more often because we used more sauce than either milk of magnesia or whiskey. Corks were carefully kept but nevertheless on many a morning there was none for the school bottle and the art of making do saw an old newspaper torn into strips and rolled up to form a makeshift stopper.

Our newspaper, the *Cork Examiner*, was a multi-purpose item. It cleaned and polished windows and it covered bare timber floors before the first lino or tarpaulin went down, thus providing underlay and insulation. Placed in layers on top of wire bed-springs, it eased the wear on the horsehair mattress; cut into the right shape, it became insoles in heavy leather boots and shoes and, later, in wellingtons when they became part of our lives. Even though it could never be described as baby soft, it was the forerunner of the multi-million-pound industry that subsequently provided soft solutions in the toilet-paper business. Rolled into balls it was a firelighter, its effectiveness improved by a sprinkling of paraffin oil. Ned shaped it into funnels and filled it with sweets to make a *tóimhsín*, as he called it.

At home it lined drawers and was considered moth-proof and, when nothing else was available, it was used as a dustpan. One of our more industrious neighbours regularly covered her potato stalks with newspaper at night and this protected them from frost.

An item used to great effect by good housekeepers was the goose wing. It was particularly useful for high-flung cobwebs, and where the wing could not reach the eye would not see. It was just as well, however, that some cobwebs remained after the goose-wing's flight because they were nature's flykillers, ready and waiting to trap the flies which had not been discouraged by the nicandra or shoo-fly we hung around the windows.

Necessity was the mother of resourcefulness and everything available was put to good use. Horse manure fortified our roses without any assistance from shop-bought preparations and garden sprays were unheard of. The suds from the washtub were used to keep slugs off the cabbage. If the tub itself leaked it could always be sealed with a mixture of curds and lime brushed into the base and allowed to harden. Leaking buckets were repaired with a "mend-it" which consisted of two little circular bits of tin with a sandwich of cork in between. One piece of the mend-it was put at each side of the leak and the two pieces were then screwed into each other, the cork acting as a sealer. Care had to be taken when hand-mixing animal foodstuffs in a bucket that had been mended in this way because the tin could pierce deeply beneath your fingernails. Travelling knights of the road repaired items that needed more skill than we possessed; they also made tin gallons which were bigger than the normal ones, though quality rather than quantity was the hallmark of their trade. Every house had a last on which shoes and boots were repaired, and on Saturday nights the children's boots were lined up for repair with iron tips and protectors, and sometimes for patching, which was done with an awl, wax and a ball of hemp.

Mending was a basic skill in our household arts, and was much relied on. Old sheets, worn down the centre where the most pressure was brought to bear, got a new lease of life from a centre-to-sides piece of surgery. When the collars of men's shirts became frayed they were still a long way from becoming dusters, because the collar was turned and the shirt salvaged though admittedly not as Sunday best anymore. Some shirts were collarless and an attachable collar was clasped into position with studs; collarless during the working week, these were what are now called grandfather shirts. My First Communion dress was a hand-me-down belonging to my sister, with a band added on around the tail because my legs were longer than hers.

We had no need of proprietary cleaning agents because our own remedies were always close at hand. If the cat did what he must where he shouldn't, turf dust was the removal agent which deodorized and eradicated all in one go. If the hens committed the same offence on the kitchen floor, a shovel of ashes from behind the open fire came into action, and ashes were also used for cleaning the silver and aluminium teapots. The bag of lime was essential for keeping things clean around the farm. During the summer months, when the animals had gone to the fields leaving their houses empty behind them, these were whitewashed and disinfected with lime.

Almost everything had more than one use. Warm covers of pots and bastables wrapped in old sheets became bed warmers, and our hot-water bottles were earthenware jars; sometimes, too, the clothes-iron was heated and wrapped up well to warm the bed on a very cold night. Cord which arrived on parcels from town was never thrown away: it was rolled up in a ball to be available for emergency service as garters, to keep up knickers if the necessity arose, or to act as a belt. Hay twine kept buttonless coats closed on cold days or secured the bottoms of wide-legged trousers against the perils of both winds and rodents.

All boxes were made of timber, and these were prized acquisitions. When Christmas supplies came in them you treated them with respect because, whether you got timber boxes, and how many you got, depended on your standing with the shopkeeper. The long double-department orange box served as two semi-detached nests in the hen-house, as did the smaller apple and orange boxes. The long orange box, stood upright, became a bedside locker and, when it was fronted with a frilly curtain, could look quite decorative. The butter box was the most solid and the most prized of all the boxes and had many uses, including those of tool box and lady's work box. It became fashionable to cover the butter box with leatherette and put a padded cushion on top, and in this way it served the dual purpose of work box and fireside seat. The five-pound cheese box held nails or other odds and ends in many houses. My mother bought our tea by the chest, and this was a large, plywood box, lined with silver paper. We stored our summer clothes in it during the winter and our winter blankets during the summer.

But the flour bag was undoubtedly the queen of all the objects that entered our house with the potential for alternative use. A soft, white cloth sack, across which was written the weight and source of the flour, it was apt, if dropped suddenly, to engulf you in white, billowing clouds, and if you travelled with it on the creamery cart you might very well come away from it with a piebald look. But once the sack was empty its reincarnation began.

The first step was to render it anonymous by removing the marks of its previous existence, the blue or red stencil which told its story. It was soaked in a tub of very hot water laced with washing soda, which soon bleached out its identity and the details of its weight – of 112 or 140 pounds. Some people ignored this eradication process and once our old friend Dan came across such a case when he was out looking for one of our horses which had strayed. He had travelled through many fields and over distant hills, searching and enquiring if anyone had seen the horse when, as he told my father later, "Jakus me, boss, I came to a little house up on the side of a hill and knocked on the door. It was opened by a fine ball of a woman in a long white nightdress with 140 pounds written across her chest." These nightdresses made from sacks were long-wearing and comfortable, but most people removed the printed statistics lest they end up on sensitive areas, either front or back.

The flour bag often became a tea-towel, in which capacity it had great absorbancy. It might also become a table-cloth, pillow-case, bed-sheet (known as the "bageen" sheet) or apron, or answer other female needs when nothing else was available. It lined children's winter clothes or became the top half of a grey flannel petticoat. It lined a patchwork quilt or, when well worn, was tied around the top of the milk churn as a strainer. The Christmas pudding was boiled in it and then wrapped in another, dry one for storage, and it was wrapped around the hot bastable cake to soften the crust.

Some of the flour bags were made of better material than others, and the flake meal came in a very good quality bag which was used for making tea-cosies which were lined inside with sheep's wool. Often they were embroidered with bright colours or the threads were drawn to create interesting designs for colourful, durable tray-cloths, dressing-table mats and runners for the tops of chests of drawers. Some artistic souls painted pictures on this fine, closely woven material.

Its uses, like its life-span, were endless. It had a soft, pleasant feel, and when put out to dry it soaked in sunshine and every country smell; the older it was the more pliable it became, making it the ideal absorber in which to wrap babies' free-flowing regions. In its old age it served as a softly caressing facecloth, or a soothing bandage to wrap up bloody cuts and support damaged limbs. During its existence it went through many transformations, until finally it was as fine as tissue-paper. So delicate and transparent was it then that I sometimes thought it could come again into another life as the gossamer wings of white butt. flies.

Of course, those who perfected the art of making do ran the risk of being regarded as thrifty to a fault. A mild enough saying was that "she could live under a hen", but if Dan was describing someone he considered to be very tight-fisted and conniving he would remark: "That one could live in your ear and rent out the other one without you knowing it".

In our house we made do, practising the art with the best of them, but somehow my father was never satisfied and we were reared to a background chant about waste and extravagance, as he constantly complained that there was enough food thrown out of our house to keep another family well fed. One day he was going on yet again about how thrifty they had all been in his young days when my sister Lucy, who could always be depended on to take the wind out of his sails, came out with the comment, "God, the dead were lucky they were buried or else ye'd have made soup out of them!"

Nell's Christmas Spirit

OLD NELL, OUR nearest and most eccentric neighbour, did not believe in Christmas. Despite all my efforts to convert her and re-introduce her to a child's view of Christmas, she stubbornly remained a non-believer. It was the one point in our relationship on which we could not reach a compromise. To me Christmas was wonderful, thrilling, magnificent, an absolute high point of the year, but Nell dismissed all my excitement and all the general fuss as a load of old rubbish. In this she was, in a way, simply being consistent: after all, she did not observe any of the rituals most of the neighbours considered to be important elements of normal life. Funerals, for example, she dismissed scathingly as "queues of crazy men following dead men".

Her main objection to Christmas centred around the question of goodwill to all men. If Nell did not feel goodwill towards you for the rest of the year she saw no reason why Christmas should change anything. What she hated above all else was the expectation that money should be spent; she had no intention of allowing Christmas to force open the brass clasp of her scruffy black purse. If other people wanted to spend money, and if Nell should happen to be at the receiving end of their generosity, that suited her fine, but she never felt the need to acknowledge gifts, still less to reciprocate; she believed in one-way traffic and that all roads should lead to Nell. Not afflicted with a sensitive nature, she accepted everything that came her way, without any sense of obligation to express or even to feel gratitude.

Shopkeepers at that time gave out Christmas presents to their best customers and Nell expected to be numbered amongst the recipients, though so meagre was her spending that she could scarcely be described as a customer at all. If she had any doubts about a shopkeeper's generosity, she presented herself at his counter a few days before Christmas. Having purchased as little as possible, she gave him a big smile. In Nell's case this could be a rather intimidating experience because her false teeth, which she wore only on special occasions, often came adrift, and when this happened she promptly whipped them out in front of the surprised shopkeeper. At this stage he felt so put out that he handed Nell the first thing available to cover her – as he imagined – embarrassment. What he failed to realize was that he was the only one feeling embarrassed, and in his ignorance he finished up giving her far more than he had intended. By the use of such tactics she succeeded in scoring very well in the Christmas stakes and it always amused her particularly when she managed to drag something out of someone who was, like herself, tight-fisted.

One Christmas Jim the hackney-man, who owned the local pub where Nell sometimes bought a bottle of whiskey to warm her at night, decided that he was not going to be bullied by her into parting with a free bottle. Having pulled every stunt, including her false teeth trick, there was still nothing doing, so finally she asked straight out: "Jim, what about my Christmas box?"

"What about it, Nell?" he answered.

"Are you forgetting it?" she asked.

"No," he replied.

"I'll take it now so," she told him, "because I might not be in again before Christmas."

"Nell," he said, looking her straight in the eye, "you don't deserve a free bottle and you're not getting it."

"Well, Jim," she said heavily, "you're a bad boyo in these festive times."

That was a bit rich coming from her, but she held no ill-feelings towards him; if he had parted with a bottle she would have enjoyed it, but when he did not she admired his astuteness in getting the better of her.

Nell allowed me to decorate her house at Christmas time, and I enjoyed doing so. At home I had to share the decorating with four sisters, and much arguing and disagreement went on, but at Nell's I had it all my own way. There was no question of her spending any money on decorations, but then we did not buy any at home either, making use of our Christmas cards and balloons which were already in the house. Nell's one Christmas expenditure was on a big red candle, so that was the centre around which I accomplished my transformation of her long, thatched house.

On the days leading up to Christmas I prepared her for the festive occasion in which she had not the slightest interest. It was a measure of her tolerance that she never objected, or else it was the fact that, having spent so much time with her and come to know her so well, I sensed instinctively just how much she would endure. The big clean-up that went on at home was definitely not possible in Nell's house. At the very mention of washing the floor and cleaning the windows she would roll her eyes to heaven.

"Child! Don't be disturbing clean dirt. My mother used to get the spade to the floor every Christmas."

And that brought that discussion to a quick standstill.

She had great respect for cobwebs, maintaining that

they possessed both practical and beautiful qualities; the evidence of her admiration was draped in every corner of the house. She regarded them as the original and best flykillers, and if the spiders had put so much creative energy into weaving them, Nell was not going to destroy the products of their artistry. When we studied the delicate threads of a new creation I had to agree with her, but I found that I did not share her enthusiasm for the furry and soot-laden specimens which hung from her rafters like so many black rags.

Christmas cards were not plentiful at home but some were quite beautiful and ours were not thrown away after Christmas but were carried forward from year to year as decorations. In a box at the bottom of a press in the parlour my mother kept these cards and I would always appropriate a few. So, on Nell's window during the festive season cards could be found which wished her and all the children a very happy Christmas. Indeed, anyone who was inquisitive enough to read the cards in Nell's house would end up completely confused, for there were loving greetings from brothers, sisters and cousins whom she simply did not have. Uninterested in communicating with anyone, she lived in an isolation which was almost complete apart from my intrusions. She would pick up some of the cards with which I had decorated her house, read their inscriptions, and snort in disgust at the stupidity of their senders.

Every year my mother invited Nell to spend Christmas with us and every year she refused. She did not believe in togetherness, preferring the quietness of her own place; as she bluntly told my mother, she could do without the aggravation of a crowd of children making noise around her. However, she usually called on Christmas Eve on her way home from confession, where she went to impress on the priest how lonely Christmas was for someone like herself – though she never tried this stunt on our veteran parish priest who knew her too well and saw through her manoeuvres. But if we had a new curate she would put on an act worthy of Siobhan McKenna and have him almost crying into his soutane. If he called to her later with something to brighten her Christmas she would say, "God bless him, wasn't he very soft? For all the learning they have, they must come to the country to be educated".

All of her strange pronouncements she made in a high-pitched, piercing wail which made it practically impossible to carry on normal conversation with her. If she was imparting to you anything that she considered to be of a confidential nature, she would warn you in a voice that everyone within half a mile could hear. "Keep that in your belly," she would say. If this conversation was taking place, as many of them did, inside at Mass, Nell's whisper would be heard all around the church, rendering the priest mere background noise.

One Christmas Eve she sat at the end of our kitchen table having tea while my mother stuffed the goose at the other end and we children sorted out decorations in between. Finally the clamour reached such a level that Nell could stand it no longer; just before heading for home she told my mother how glad she was that she had not inflicted on herself the persecutions that my mother had to bear – namely her children. Nell's particular way of expressing how she had come to be so lucky was, "Thanks be to God that I never felt the need of a man in my bed". Men were in general, as far as Nell was concerned, the begetters of a wide variety of undesirable after-effects.

On the following day, just as we sat down to our Christmas dinner, Nell tore in the door, demanding in her piercing wail, "Did ye find my teeth?"

"Your false teeth?" my mother enquired in some

amazement.

"Yes!" she shrieked at full volume. "When I looked at the jampot on the dresser this morning it was empty, and you know my teeth are always inside there except when I'm going out."

"But Nell," asked my mother in a soothing voice, "what makes you think that they're here?"

"Because when I was having the tea yesterday evening I took them out. They were getting stuck in that cake and could have choked me," Nell shouted, determined not to be soothed.

"Holy Christ," my father prayed at this stage, but before he could launch into his "if ever a man suffered" routine my mother interrupted.

"Nell, when I was tidying up last night your teeth were not on the table; so you must have taken them with you," she said.

"No," Nell insisted, and then her eye fell on the still-sizzling and golden goose which was lying in state at the centre of the table, and she pointed her black finger at it. "That's where they are!" she shouted in excitement as if she had been struck by divine inspiration. "They must have got mixed up with the sliced onions because I remember seeing a dish of them near me and they are gone into the goose with the stuffing."

"Mother of God!" my father started again, and this time there was no way my mother was going to stop him. "That's all I need now for my Christmas dinner – Nell's gnashers grinning out at me through the arse of the goose!"

"Nell," said my mother firmly, "if we find them we'll bring them back to you, or would you like to stay for dinner?"

"Stay for dinner," cried Nell, "and eat my own false teeth!" And with that she departed, banging the door after her.

"Dear God," my father breathed, "but she is one galvanized hoor!" He seldom used what my mother termed "farmyard language" in the house, but where Nell was concerned his patience quickly reached breaking point.

After Nell's departure we all sat horror-stricken, gazing at our golden goose which a few minutes earlier had had our mouths watering but which now apparently held an appalling secret. It seemed a tragedy had intervened to cast a shadow over our young lives. Normally the goose filled with our mother's beautiful potato stuffing was one of the highlights of Christmas, but Nell had certainly snuffed out that light with the prospect of what might lie within.

My mother had a simple approach to the sticky situation. "I will dish out all the stuffing and then we will know one way or the other," she said. So she carved the goose and dished out the stuffing from both ends. Because there were many mouths to be fed our goose had no unfilled cavities and was stuffed to capacity in all departments. As my mother spooned out the stuffing we all watched intently and it was one of the few occasions on which silence had ever prevailed at our table. Even my father, apart from an occasional appeal to the Lord to witness his suffering, saw it all through in silent apprehension. Finally the last spoonful proved that we were in the clear and we all cheered, relieved that the horror of Nell's teeth had been lifted from our minds. And because we had come so close to losing it, the dinner tasted all the more luscious. Our dogs would never know how close they had come to enjoying a full Christmas dinner.

Later that evening I went across the fields to Nell with a plate of dinner wrapped in a tea-towel. The countryside had a special stillness and I watched my breath fuse into the cold, crisp air. The water in the *glaise* looked black against the grey, frosty grass and the cow tracks, frozen hard, bore a multiplicity of designs. As I jumped between them Nell's dinner cooled in the freezing early night air. Feeling no need to hurry, however, I ambled along and finally arrived at Nell's house at my ease, to find her sitting by a big fire surrounded by her dogs and cats. From her chair by the fire she had viewed through her kitchen window my progress across the fields.

"Child," she said, "you took your time. My dinner will be frozen."

She put the wrapped plate on a black pot by the fire and the dogs and cats jostled for position to sniff at it. I lay down on Nell's old timber settle, dislodging some of her cats who had made it their bed. I admired the redberry holly I had placed above it where it contrasted vividly with the black rafters. I decided that all in all Nell's kitchen wore a festive air, despite her reluctance to be part of the season that was with us. The red candle flickering on the window and the yellow flames of the turf fire filled the room with a warm glow. The colourful Christmas cards stood on the deep window-sill and between the brown lustre jugs and bowls on the dark dresser. The stillness of the room was disturbed only by the tick-tock of the old seven-day wall clock and the hissing of resin from the logs as the flames of the burning sods licked around them. It was then that I saw, out of the corner of my eye, grinning whitely in the shadows, the false teeth resting in the jampot which held them more often than Nell's mouth. How long had they been there? For some reason I did not ask her.

Goody, Goody

GOODY WAS A balm to bruised minds and bodies and held a special place in all our hearts. Mothers made it when we were feeling sick, but not sick enough for medicine and definitely not needing the doctor – maybe feeling just a little out of step with our fellow human beings and in need of loving or the knowledge that somebody loved us. It was a simple but effective antidote to all ills and was within the scope of all budgets.

Tufts of white bread were plucked from a thick cut or a well-padded heel of a loaf to line the bottom of a cup or a basin, depending on the size of the consumer. Some dressers boasted a colourful, flowery basin which was reserved especially for making goody. On top of the foundation layer of bread came a generous shake of sugar, and sweet-toothed people turned the sugar bowl sideways and poured freely. Then another covering of bread was added, and more sugar, and so on, layer upon layer until it rose, dome-like, over the rim.

While this tiered miracle was being created a wary eye was kept on a saucepan of milk heating on a rake-out of hot coals by the fire. You forgot it at your peril; if you took your eye off it for one second it could erupt in billowing bubbles and overflow onto the fire, scattering ashes and filling the kitchen with an acrid smell. Experienced goody makers managed to get the two jobs to reach completion simultaneously. Then the boiling milk was poured gently in a circular motion over the soft, spongy bread and sugar, which sank with a subdued sigh beneath the scalding waterfall. Some discerning people liked to hold back the skim at the top of the milk, which might be flecked with turf dust and ashes, while other, less fastidious souls let it all pour in. Then, with a big spoon, the entire concoction was squelched up and down, the spoon making a slurping passage through the goody to meet the bottom of the bowl with a dull thud. As the mixing progressed the goody cooled and the connoisseur knew when the precise point for satisfying expectant taste-buds had been reached. Thus was created a soft, sweet, creamy bowl of delicious, slushy sedation.

With this soothing, seductive mush babies were weaned off the breast and introduced to solid food. In later years the goody was there when no other comfort was available. Many a hardened bachelor, long in the tooth, coming home on a cold day from the fair and having no welcoming arms to erase the memory of a bad bargain, found his solace in a basin of hot goody. His blood chilled by a long trudge up a mountainy road with a cold wind whipping around his ears, he was rejuvenated and reheated by this bowl of warm comfort. Often an overly discerning lady, unwilling to wrinkle her linen sheets with what she considered the unsuitable manhood available, took a china cup of consoling goody to see her through the night. Happy couples, too, having bedded down their young after a hectic day, shared a bowl of warm goody before going on to share greater comforts. Then, in old age, when sensitive molars could send searing pain through brittle jaws, goody gently weaned them off solid fare with its delicate touch.

Chewing, which rocked unsteady teeth in their shrunken rooting ground, was no longer necessary as goody slid effortlessly over flawed masticators.

Goody was a source of consolation for all seasons. It was an infantile soother, a male menopause stress-reliever, a female oestrogen replacer and, in old age, the last comfort against the ravages of time.

Cow Time

COME THE FIRST glimmer of light and the slight twitter that introduced the dawn chorus, the cock crew loud and clear. I imagined that he must sleep with one eye half open in case he might miss that little splinter of light in the dark sky. He was our alarm clock and his cock-crow was a call to arms and a salutation to the new day. There was nothing half-hearted or hesitant about it: his "cock-a-doodle-do" rang out bright and clear. The vibrant call cut through waves of muzzy sleepiness and was repeated every five minutes until the cock was assured that the coming of the dawn was not going to be ignored by those who lacked the sense of occasion he possessed.

He was a fine-looking fellow, with a bright red cock's-comb which contrasted dramatically with his snow-white feathers. His long, strong, yellow legs spread into gripping claws and he had a vicious beak; he used both beak and claws to keep his huge harem in submission. He strolled arrogantly around the farmyard and occasionally during the day he perched himself on top of a dunghill or on a shed and crowed out his superiority over his flock which was now scattered around the haggard and farmyard.

Our first job after answering the cock's morning call was to bring in the cows. They had no built-in mechanism like the cock's to tell them that the time had come to head home for milking. Usually they were spread out around the field, some grazing, some lying down contentedly chewing the cud. They rose at their own pace when they saw you coming and meandered towards the gap. Rounding up cows in the early morning was a soothing experience. They looked at you out of large, moist, trusting eyes and obediently complied with whatever it was you wanted them to do. As you walked along behind their swinging tails they exuded a warm contentment with their lot that was contageous. The rhythm of their gait compelled you to slow to the relaxed pace of their bovine world. Arriving in the stall yard, each went to her own stall and put her head into her own place. While the sleepy-headed milkers arrived, some of whom were perpetually bad-tempered in the morning, the cows stood impassively chewing the cud, with faraway looks in their big eyes as if dreaming of green fields and mossy streams. With their long tails they flicked away annoying flies.

We had three cowhouses or stalls, and they were known as the new stalls, the middle stalls and the old stalls. The new and middle stalls had grain lofts over them and these my father had built. The old stalls, however, had been there for many generations in a lovely old stone building which was partly covered with ivy and had deep, narrow windows and a cobbled floor. Here in the crevices between the stones the swallows nested and swished in and out above the cows' heads and in the straw loft overhead at the peak of each rafter were rows of nests.

The milkers went to their own stalls and milked their own cows. There was never a worked-out arrangement about who was to milk any particular cow: the system just evolved whereby certain people liked to milk certain cows and that was it. The full buckets of warm milk were carried out of the stalls and across the yard to the stand where twenty-gallon churns stood on a concrete base, and into these the milk was poured and strained through a white muslin cloth tied around the top of each churn. My father left the stalls early to catch the pony and have his breakfast. Pony tackled to the creamery cart, it was backed in beside the stand and the covered churns were rolled into it.

When the cows had been milked and let out again the only other job that was usually done before breakfast was feeding the calves. They were by now bellowing their heads off: having heard the rattle of the milk buckets, they knew that breakfast time had come. All the small calves were individually fed and each one would be at a different milk strength; there were calves on pure fresh milk, calves on a mixture of fresh and sour, and calves on sour milk only, and bearing in mind each calf's requirements was a bit like preparing the feeding bottles in a hospital nursery.

Before opening the door of the house to feed them you had to be thoroughly organized as their bucket manners were not well cultivated and each had just one aim in life: to get its head into a bucket, any bucket. Sometimes you might finish up with two heads in one bucket and a spare bucket with no head in it. But to get a calf's head out once it was in was almost impossible, as the only lever you had to pull them by was their ears and, pull as you might, this had no effect. When the calves were finally matched with their correct feed, the bucket had to be held firmly while the calf was drinking because calves had a strange habit of butting with their heads, almost as an expression of appreciation. They could turn the bucket upside down or, worse still, give you a pair of black and blue shin-bones as a result of a belt of a bucket.

After wrestling with the calves we took a break and fed ourselves. When breakfast was over the rest of the morning jobs were done, but somehow they never seemed to take as long as the evening ones, which was strange because the routine was almost exactly the same.

In the summer, as soon as the first evening shadows stretched their slanting fingers across the fields, all the animals converged on the farmyard. Hungry animals are noisy animals and the only ones who were not hungry were the cows but they bellowed too because they wanted to be milked. The demanding clamour could be deafening. Permanently stationed in the yard was a house of pigs in for fattening and they now gave off a shrill, demented scream as they jumped against their door and rattled their empty iron trough around the house. In the next few houses baby bonhams might be squealing for their mothers who had been out eating grass and rolling in mud. Two large gates led from the fields into the yard and these were closed at this point to bring a bit of law and order to the situation. Outside one gate the big calves, who had spent their day out in the fields, were now bellowing for their supper with long, plaintive maa-maa-maa sounds that went on non-stop. Outside the other gate the returning sows screeched with continuous determination. Already in the yard were hens, turkeys, ducks and chickens, all adding to the chaotic chorus of wailing animals and birds. It was pure and absolute bedlam.

First to be dealt with were the hens, because they were everywhere, jumping into the other animals' feed and scurrying around between your feet, so you had to get rid of them first. A bucket of oats was taken to the front of their house and a call of "tioc, tioc" brought them clustering after you. The oats were scattered on the ground and they pecked it up. Next came the ducks, who would actually eat anything, which my father maintained was the reason why their eggs were not up to the same standard as the hens' eggs. The turkeys, however, were a finicky lot and the baby turkeys were actually fed on scrambled eggs and nettles. Sometimes they got a strange complaint called the gapes and then they were put under a cardboard box where a pink powder was blown around them. Turkeys were delicate and demanding, but the turkey-cock was a colourful old boy who would fan out his bright feathers and huge wings and dance sideways like an excited matador going into attack. And attack he would, because he was an aggressive devil and would fly at you with wings spread out in full flight.

The fowl quietened, the background wailing still continued and the pigs were the next to be tackled and reduced to comparative silence. In the yard was the "mess house", as it was called, but no serried ranks of soldiers dined in this place where the pigs' mess was mixed in a timber tub with a long-handled shovel. Ration was shovelled out of jute bags, mixed with water to a sloppy consistency, and then taken in buckets to the pigs. Facing into a house full of hungry pigs required a certain amount of courage, brute force and timing, and the timing was the most important element. Hungry pigs shrieked and jumped at the door in waves, and the trick was to get in the door and reach the trough while they were still between waves, building up for a renewed assault. If you did not get your timing right they could take the legs from under you and then you would emerge highly perfumed with a concentrated essence and pure toilet water. The home-coming sows outside the gate were now screaming to high heaven and trying to lift the gate out of the way with their snouts while their bonhams, hearing them, squealed in hunger, but once they were let in the noise died down.

The calves now provided the final chorus. An iron trough set in a cement base was used to feed them and iron dividers separated each head. The trough was filled with sour milk, which had been brought home earlier from the creamery and stored in two large tar-barrels in the corner of the yard. The milk was drawn by bucket from the barrel until the trough was full and then you opened the gate and stood well back to avoid being knocked down in the ensuing stampede. Some-times the bigger calves were held back for a few minutes to give the small ones a chance to get a head start. Once fed, the calves went back to the fields.

The peace that descended on the farmyard when all the demanding, clamouring animals had finally been fed was emphasized by the volume of the noise that had preceded it. It was such a relief to have them all quietened down that you could almost feel the silence. This daily routine was called simply "doing the jobs" and in some ways was separate from the milking which, because it involved so many more people, was con-sidered the biggest event of the day.

During the summer many of the farm buildings were empty by night. The cows were "out on grass" from early summer to late autumn – how late depended on the weather – and the horses only used the stables in the winter. The farmyard late of a summer's evening had a whispering life. Swallows swished in and out through the open doors and the farm cats stretched out in the mangers, where the horses would not tolerate them during the winter. Pigs, normally curled up together for warmth, now lay far apart to keep cool in their warm houses, giving little grunts and snorts as if reliving memories of rolling in cool mud. An occasional muted quack came from the duck-house and even the trouble-some turkeys chirped quietly to themselves. The hens, sitting in rows on their perches in the whitewashed hen-house, gave occasional clucks and gurgles before bury-ing their heads under their wings. Even his majesty the cock was taking it easy, sitting on the top perch and keeping a beady eye on his rows of ladies-in-waiting.

The Missioners

THE MISSIONERS WHO thundered into the parish church most summers were to us as exciting as a travelling roadshow. We loved these tall, graceful men in long, sweeping black gowns whose black, sectioned birettas clung precariously to their polls and whose giant wooden rosary beads clanked around them like horses' traces. They were larger than life and we saw them as visitors from another world – a world of incense, long, polished corridors and continuous prayer. To me the missioner on the altar provided a one-man entertainment, which was all the more exciting when he strode back and forth shouting; it was high drama, and better again when he thumped the altar. Usually coming in pairs, these missioners generally comprised one quiet, holy one and a cross, dramatic fellow. Different orders had different levels of ferocity but we preferred the fire and brimstone brigade.

There was a great sense of togetherness in the parish during the mission week. We all shared the same schedule, as farm activity had to be wound up early in the evening so that everybody could converge on the church. If you were late you might be left standing outside and miss some of the excitement or, worse still, the free missioner of the night might come around to the back door and march you up along the church until he found a seat for you. He pretended he was doing you a

51

good turn but in actual fact both he and you knew he was not.

In backyards around the town ponies and traps were tied up and bicycles were lined against the church railings. Young children living near the church had great fun stealing rides at breakneck speed down the high hill on the bikes of mountainy bachelors who did not have the filling of a trap for the mission.

Up one side of the churchyard, against the iron railings, was a long row of mission stalls called "standings", from which holy pictures, statues, holy-water fonts, rosary beads and a wide and varied selection of medals, some with encased relics, were sold. Anything thought to have the power to cultivate devotion was available and the items were international in origin but not, of course, interdenominational. We savoured our examination of everything on offer and adorned ourselves with anything that could be pinned or hung on. We hung brown and green scapulars around our necks, and Blessed Martin and Saint Jude competed with each other for pride of place on our woollen vests, but as Blessed Martin's was the first black face I had ever seen I felt protective towards him, in case he might feel lost in this strange place, so he was always first into my safety-pin. The general favourite was St Christopher bearing the Child on his back, perhaps because everybody felt the need of a St Christopher to carry them over the rough patches of life.

The colourful statues stood in rows high on the back shelves of the stalls. We studied the different facial expressions: the soft, pleading eyes of Our Lady; the dark, inscrutable ones of St Theresa. But the cherub-faced Child of Prague was my favourite because I liked his happy look. Various statues of the Child of Prague came into our house over the years but always they lost their heads and we had all sorts of strange beliefs concerning him. We believed that it was lucky if his head fell off; also, that he liked a prominent position, being averse to hovering in the background; and if you wanted a fine day you put him out the night before. I believed that there was a logic of sorts to everything and supposed that the reason for this was that the draught would catch him when he was left out overnight and he would need the sun the following day. Anyway, all the sideshows and their attendant beliefs and stories had the welcome effect of adding colour to the mission and enhancing our appreciation of it.

Like most children, I relished ideals, and the higher the better. So the mission to me was a big spiritual clean-up, a bit like getting the house ready for the Stations, only this time the house was within my mind's four walls. My heart bled at the sermon on the passion and I felt I could identify with Christ carrying his cross along the hot, dusty road to Calvary. I felt so sorry for Our Lady, pregnant and tired on that cold winter's night, riding on the donkey into Bethlehem. But the missioners lost me when they came to the sins of the flesh and waxed eloquent in explaining the finer details of the sixth and ninth commandments. It was all so complicated that I wondered what on earth they were talking about.

One night, after a sermon distinguished by a tirade on sins in marriage which had me absolutely fascinated, trying to figure out how such sins could be achieved, we gave a lift home in the pony and trap to a woman who lived near us.

"That man tonight," she announced, "wants to take all the fun out of life."

My mother at this point tried to change the subject, surrounded as she was by children of varying ages, all of whom were listening with open mouths.

"For God's sake," the neighbour continued blithely,

"what else have Mick and I to pass the long winter's nights." She threw back her head and laughed heartily, slapping my father on the back, but this time my mother was determined that enough was enough and turned the conversation firmly in another direction.

The mission continued for a week, and to each of us it meant different things. My friend Ann spent the entire week sitting in the front seat of the upstairs gallery aiming spits on the bald heads of the men below. My father was once the victim of her marksmanship and threatened that he would dry her spit if she dared try again; religious toleration did not extend to wet insults landing on my father's bald head. Ann was full of bright ideas on how to make life more exciting. Long queues formed for confession, which was part of the spiritual clean-up operation of the mission. We young ones had a special time set aside for us and once when the missioner was late my friend decided that action was required to relieve the boredom. She posted a look-out at the door and sat into the confessional to hear our confessions herself. We took turns going in on either side and telling the most atrocious sins we could think of. Suddenly there was a warning call from the door and we all scattered – all but the girl on the right-hand side of the box who, because she was furthest from the door and the sound was deadened by the heavy baize cloth of the confessional, did not realize that the missioner had replaced Ann. When the grille of the confessional was drawn back, thinking in the dark that it was her friend, she stuck her finger into the missioner's eye. We discovered that day that even holy men knew how to use strong language.

The mission closed with a grand finale. It took place on a Sunday evening when, cows milked, calves and pigs fed and the resulting farmyard aromas eradicated, we all headed for the church. Women arrived laden with lumpy parcels almost as if they had done their Christmas shopping. The stalls did a roaring trade now as this was the last opportunity to get something and have it blessed by the missioners.

The church was thronged to the utmost because anybody who had not come voluntarily to the mission had been visited by the missioner and a speedy conversion had been effected, so tonight they were all in except those we considered the real lost causes. The main aisle, which was reserved for men, was packed to capacity, and some brave bodies overflowed into the the mortuary, which was normally reserved for single, laid out occupancy but which now offered standing room only. The confession boxes provided more comfortable accommodation – too comfortable in some cases because a gentle snore could sometimes be heard from them when proceedings proved particularly lengthy. The women's aisles to the right and left of the altar were a sea of colour as many a devout woman overflowing with missionary fervour crowned it with a new hat or sometimes even a complete new outfit. Sexual segregation did not rise to the three galleries where the steps as well as the seats were lined with people. The less enthusiastic took refuge on the gallery stairs and it was not unknown for a game of cards to be quietly played.

Gleaming brass candelabras bore dozens of tall lighted candles, their heavy waxen odour blending with the spicy incence from the swinging thurible. Rows of altar boys in bright red soutanes flanked the two missionaries in their gathered white surplices. Children overflowed into the aisles and sat around the altar-rails while the choir in full volume filled the church with organ music and Latin hymns. We said the rosary and were given a mixed grill of a sermon which recapped on every aspect of the previous week, and then, with everybody bearing a lighted candle, we renewed our baptismal vows. We drowned the devil in holy water and buried him in candle-grease, and evicted him out of sight back down into hell.

Mad Saints

THE KITCHEN WINDOW was broken one night when my mother and father were at the mission. Nobody saw it happen and nobody in the house was at fault, and the lack of explanation annoyed my father more than if there had been a culprit on whom he could have vented his anger. To make matters worse, the mission already had him in a bad temper because it demanded of him for the sake of peace a shut mouth, and this he found difficult to maintain. He went and listened to the missioners but the wry, caustic comments which occasionally escaped from him made clear to us that he was not overly impressed by them and only the fact that my mother took the mission so seriously prevented him from giving full expression to his opinion.

Wet days not suitable for farm work were repair and maintenance days, and so it was raining when he arrived home from the creamery with a big new pane of glass wrapped in dripping newspapers. He propped the glass carefully against the kitchen press, voicing long, detailed ultimatums regarding the fate of anyone chancing to come within half a mile of it. Having lectured all of us about the seriousness and delicacy of the job in hand, he proceeded to remove the broken glass.

Our old friend Bill sat by the fire with a few of us balanced on each knee, telling us funny stories while the two sheepdogs lay stretched out drying themselves in front of the open fire. Normally dogs were not permitted this comfort but, as my mother had gone to the morning mission and must have been delayed, we had taken advantage of her absence and let them in. The sight of easy-going Bill, the dogs and the gang of noisy children cluttering up the kitchen did nothing to soothe my father's frayed nerves. We regularly told my mother that she should have married Bill instead of my father because then we could have done as we liked. As Bill did not believe in work my father's answer to this was, "You'd all have died with the hunger".

Painstakingly he removed the broken glass from the lower pane of the window, just as he had done many times before, as this particular pane stood right in our favourite line of fire. Now we kept clear of his end of the kitchen lest we might trigger a calamity. Things proceeded calmly enough and, having removed the glass, my father kneaded the putty in his hands, which seemed to have a soothing effect on him.

A wet day in the country was conducive to visiting the neighbours, and restless spirits set to wandering. So it was that Dan could always be counted on to choose such a day on which to turn up. Knocking being a formality he never deemed necessary, he simply walked in the door accompanied, as usual, by his huge mongrel, an animal of such mixed ancestry that it scarcely merited the term dog. Our own dogs normally treated this excuse of a mutt with contempt and completely ignored him, but the sight of him strolling into the inner sanctum of the kitchen, where they themselves were seldom allowed to stretch before the fire, was more than they could tolerate. They shot into action and in the ensuing tangle of dogs, locked together in a vicious, snarling ball of legs, heads and tails, they careered around the kitchen scattering everything in sight including my father's carefully propped-up pane of glass. It broke into smithereens and sprayed around the floor in a thousand fragments like a shower of solid raindrops.

Fighting dogs are a danger to interfering hands and limbs but anger disperses all caution and my father, with a few well-placed kicks of his strong leather boot, evicted the scrapping dogs out through the gaping window. Into the aftermath of this chaos sailed my mother, who had just walked home from the mission. So imbued was she with religious zeal that she failed to register our situation. Without even taking time to remove her coat she announced in a surprised and wondering voice, "The missioner this morning said a strange thing. He said that if our ignorance and insanity did not save us we would all be damned."

"In that case," thundered my father, "there is no fear of us, because if it's ignorance and insanity that's necessary for salvation then this house is full of saints." And, catching his cap, he made for the door saying, "As a matter of fact, woman, you're standing on holy ground."

The Eternal Flame

THE VERY LARGE open fire which stretched across one end of the kitchen was the central point of the life of our home, and our family activities and gatherings all revolved around it. At its base a deep ash hole in the floor was covered over by an iron grid shaped to fit into the top of the hole, and an underground tunnel ran from the hole to the base of an upright iron bellows which stood on the right of the fire. A person sitting beside it in a comfortable *súgán* chair could turn the handle of the bellows, sending a draught along the tunnel and under the fire. The faster the wheel was turned, the brighter the fire would glow, but if handled too roughly the strap around the wheel could slip off and bring the whole proceedings to a standstill. As children we hated being landed with this awkward job. If the bellows was out of balance the strap would slip continuously and become a source of great annoyance; indeed, one of our neighbours, who was not renowned for his patience, found this so frustrating that he hit his iron bellows a belt of a sledgehammer and broke it into smithereens.

Over the fire and extending a few feet on either side of it was a huge chimney, and if you leaned in over the bellows and looked up you could see the sky. Smaller chimneys from other rooms joined it as it rose towards the roof-top, like a big river being joined by tributaries.

Directly behind the fire the wall was black from years of smoke but on either side of this black area the hob was pure white, because whitewashing the hob with lime was one of the regular Saturday jobs in the house. A black iron crane stood on one leg to the left of the fire, a long arm extending from it, and half-way along that arm another one hung down and curved to form a hook at the bottom. From this arm swung the hangers to hold the various pots and kettles over the flames. The crane was operated by a long handle which curved into a smooth knob and the hangers could be eased up and down or the whole crane, which was on a swivel, could be swung forward, leaving the heat behind it.

Two heavy iron kettles provided boiling water: the larger of the two was always called the tea kettle, while the smaller one was reserved for less prestigious uses. When a kettle was brought to the boil over the fire the cover would dance up and down giving out a whistling noise and we would call to our mother that the kettle was singing. She was very fussy when it came to making tea: she never took anybody's word that the kettle had actually boiled but had to see for herself; then, when she had made the tea, she set the teapot to draw on a few red coals known as *gríosach*.

Accompanying the two kettles was a pair of black, three-legged iron pots. The larger one was used for boiling the potatoes and the smaller one for the meat and vegetables. They were hung from the crane by the pot-hangers which hooked into the iron ears beneath their protruding upper rim, and they were covered by a heavy iron lid with a raised handle on top. To lift off the lid when it was hot the long iron tongs was sometimes used and saved many a person from scalds or burns. These two pots were used daily but they had a bigger brother which was used for Monday's washing of clothes and for Saturday-night baths. The baby of the pot family was the skillet, in which the porridge or gruel was cooked overnight in gentle heat by the fire.

Another companion of this set of pots was the bastable, which was about one-third the depth of the others and had straight sides. Its design struck me as less interesting since it lacked the generous curves which had given rise to the descriptive term "pot-bellied", but it played an important role in the house, being used for baking bread. When it had been nicely warmed it was either greased or floured and a large round cake of bread was laid to rest inside it; the cover was securely settled on top to keep out ashes and hot turf dust, and then on the outer circle of the cover a ring of red-hot coals or *cíoráns* were placed.

My mother, being a night person, was usually the last to leave the kitchen, and so it was she who generally "kindled" the fire. She raked it out and put the red coals to the side, and then covered them with hot ashes. Without a draught beneath them the *gríosach* did not light up but kept the "seed" of the fire alive so that in the morning they were still red. The first person up in the morning removed the cover from the ash hole, emptied out the ashes with a cracked cup, which gave a dull, hollow sound as it scraped off the fire bricks, and made sure that the small underground tunnel to the bellows was clear. Having raked out the still warm ashes at the side of the fire, the hot *gríosach* was put on top of the grid which had been replaced over the hole.

The materials for starting up the fire again were usually stored overnight in a box at a safe distance from the fire but drying out in its warmth. We children were often sent out to gather a *gabháil* of *cipíns* or of "roots", which were not as defined in the dictionary but were rather what my mother termed "the limbs of trees". These we cracked across our knees or split with a hatchet to render them into more manageable proportions.

THE ETERNAL FLAME

On top of the *gríosach* were placed balls of dry hay,
then *cipíns*, then the previous day's cinders and finally
cioráns, which were broken sods of turf. Then the
bellows was turned gently to fan the small red "seed" of
the fire and the hay gave off a rich aromatic smell as it
smouldered into flame, filling the kitchen with its spicy
essence. Once the fire got going sods of black turf were
put standing up around it like a guard of honour and
soon the yellow flames licked around them. Then the
ashes from the previous day's fire were shovelled into
an old tin bucket which had been retired from carrying
liquids, and the area around the hearth was brushed
clean. The fire was ready for another day.

The entire household revolved around the fire, which
provided warmth, cooking facilities and a social centre
around which we gathered at night to chat or to read.
My father had his own particular chair to the right of
the fire beside the bellows and it was his job to turn the
wheel to keep the fire glowing. Behind the bellows a
cricket often chirped, making its own contribution to
our conversations. To my father's left and under the oil
lamp sat my mother, usually darning or patching, for it
was a continual struggle to keep six pairs of childish
heels, knees and elbows from breaking out. To the left
of the fire stretched a long timber stool or form on which
we children sat in a row, feet swinging above the floor.
The chair next to our form belonged to our nearest
neighbour and daily visitor, Bill, and other chairs in the
circle were occupied by older members of the family or
other visiting neighbours. If the circle of people became
too big and we ran out of chairs, another timber form,
which seated three or four depending on their circum-
ferences, was brought into service from inside the
kitchen table.

Family hygiene also depended on the fire because
every Saturday night the big twenty-gallon pot of boil-

ing water bubbled over it and the washing commenced of an assortment of little bodies which were encased in the mud, grass, earth, hay dust and chaff that perfumed our daily lives like our own country version of *eau de cologne*. Our hair was fine-combed to evict the tenants of our time, for if this was not done on a regular basis then they established squatters' rights and proved highly undesirable lodgers. On Monday morning the big pot again came into action for the weekly wash-day, which took a full day's hard labour because keeping clean was no easy job in the country.

From the kitchen fire came the "seeds" to light the other fires in the house. A big, battered farmyard shovel, minus the handle, was filled with blazing *gríosach* and carried, a whirl of smoke behind it, at a lively pace into the parlour. It was also used to carry the seeds to upstairs bedrooms and later I would lie in bed listening to the fire crackling and watching the figures of light and shade dancing up the walls and across the low ceiling.

The kitchen fire stood at the centre of our lives, an eternal flame never to be quenched. Only when houses were finally abandoned were their kitchen fires allowed to die, and when one of our neighbours built a new house he carried the seed of the fire across the haggard in a bucket from the old house to the new. The fire was the heart of every home and its warm glow was never extinguished while people still lived in the house.

Always On
A Monday

AN ENORMOUS WOMAN – in circumference rather than height – Bridgie came every Monday to do the washing. Great rolls of flesh were restrained within her cross-over navy overall, the straps of which disappeared into deep furrows; safety-pins glinted in rows on her bosom like medals on a soldier's chest. So intense was the pressure on the overall to cover her vast higher regions that it could not succeed in reaching her knees. She never wore stockings and her heavy legs curved neither in nor out but seemed to have been poured straight down into her men's boots. Her too-tight jumper just covered her elbows, below which large hands brought everything and everybody surrounding her under her control, and often she caught me by the scruff of my neck to get me out of her way. The hair which inadequately covered her head defied restraint, sticking out like straw in a variety of colours induced by her habit of rinsing it regularly in cold tea.

Above all else Bridgie's teeth set her apart from ordinary mortals. Each tooth went its own way with no particular collective direction in mind, and the top row lacked any sense of togetherness at all. Her dental arrangements enabled Bridgie to accomplish something which would otherwise have been impossible: both a non-stop talker and a chain smoker, she was able to park a cigarette between two top teeth and continue

talking without a break. There it remained smouldering away until Bridgie remembered it and it flared back
into life again as she gave it a gigantic pull. Sometimes,
however, she forgot the parked cigarette and lit another
one: then we would dance around her shouting with
delight, "Bridgie, Bridgie, you've two chimneys smok-
ing!" Her answer to this was to snort "Shit!" in frustra-
tion and fling the old butt into the fire. My mother
forbade us to adopt Bridgie's rough vocabulary but she
dared not try to curtail Bridgie's own colourful flow of
words, for the vibrations of her wrath could shake the
very foundations of the house.

Early on Monday morning the big twenty-gallon pot
was hung over the fire and filled with water and by the
time Bridgie arrived it was sending steam signals up
the chimney. Seasonal weather variations had no effect
on her outfit and the only concession she made to
extreme cold was to don a pair of hand-knitted grey
socks that she turned down over the tops of her black
boots. She threw a well-worn tweed coat over her
shoulders; as it fell short of the overall it afforded scant
shelter, but she maintained that "only the too thin and
the too lazy feel the cold".

On arrival she made a pot of black tea and had a fag
before commencing operations, sorting out the clothes
into different heaps. As she sorted she gave a running
commentary on the clothes – though it could equally
have been on their owners. Catching up a very dirty pair
of pants she would exclaim, "Ah, you dirty bastard!" and
coming to the whites she might hold up a nightdress and
declare, "You little strap: another wear would do you no
harm".

She would grasp one of the strong timber *súgán*
chairs and slap it face downwards on its front legs with
its top wedged against the table and lift the big timber
wash-tub onto its back. Sometimes she placed two

chairs facing each other and put the tub on their laps. With a tin gallon she ladled steaming water from the black pot into an iron bucket which she carried across the kitchen and poured into the tub; then she added cold water which she drew in buckets from the stream at the end of the garden, where water ran through a pipe we called the spout. When she was satisfied that the temperature was right she put on her bag apron and set to work on the clothes. She caught up one of the bundles, threw it into the tub and rammed the clothes down under the water with the legs of the timber washboard. Not content merely to wash the clothes, she attacked them, banging them onto the ridged washboard and plastering them onto it with a large block of red or white carbolic soap; then she scrubbed each offending garment up and down with great ferocity. And while she worked she would talk, sing or curse, depending on her prevailing humour.

As she washed the clothes over the ridged surface of the washboard clouds of steam enveloped Bridgie and the glow of her cigarette was like a beacon in the misty kitchen. She squeezed the clothes by hand, rinsed and squeezed again. Meanwhile, the pot was kept full and boiling over the fire as tub after tub of washing was piled high on the table. Sheets and whites got an extra final rinse in blue, which came in a little round solid block in a muslin bag, to give them the blue-white look.

Wash-day took over the entire kitchen, filling it with a soapy, steamy smell. Sometimes some of the whites were boiled in the big black pot and as they were lifted out with the handle of a brush they sent steam billowing upwards and turned the kitchen into a danger-zone of fog from which Bridgie barred children and males alike, considering both species to lack sufficient intelligence to avoid being scalded alive. To us the kitchen at this point offered the delight of paddling around barefoot in the copious water on the floor but Bridgie always saw us off declaring, "Get out of my way or I'll catch you by the hasp of your arse and hang you off the clothes-line with the washing". Her knowledge of the human anatomy sometimes sent us off to our mother to enquire the meaning of new words, and my mother often had a hard time trying to come up with explanations.

When early summer came Bridgie found a use for us: we became the agitators and danced barefoot on the blankets when she gave them all a lukewarm tub wash. The heavy, pure wool Foxford and Dripsey blankets harboured many a flea in comfortable conditions until evil-smelling yellow Keating's powder put a stop to their jump. Bridgie traced the genealogy of the flea back to the fact that "Adam had 'em", and she taught us a little verse which we chanted together as we danced up and down in her tub of warm, soapy blankets:

Big fleas
Have little fleas
Upon their backs
To bite them
And little fleas
Have littler fleas
And so ad infinitum.

Summer washing was done out in the garden near the spout where there was a plentiful supply of cold water, and then it was the hot water that had to be drawn from the kitchen. Bridgie ordered us to keep away from the wash-tub when it was full of water, but we had a game we played in the tub when her back was turned which we called "doggie sail away": we floated two bits of stick across the tub and the first stick to reach the other side was the winner. One day while Bridgie was in the kitchen my sister Clare and I leaned across the raised tub urging on our contestants. Suddenly Clare lost her balance and went head first under the water, legs waving over the edge of the tub. I was so shocked that when I opened my mouth to scream no sound came out. I ran towards the kitchen, and when Bridgie saw my ashen face she made immediately for the tub, cursing and praying at the same time as she manoeuvered her considerable bulk as fast as she could down the garden. At the tub she quickly hauled out Clare who, after a certain amount of coughing and spluttering, soon recovered. For weeks after this episode Bridgie kept us at a safe distance from her tub and warned us, "Don't come within a donkey's roar of me ye bloody little brats!"

In time she forgave us for the fright we had given her and allowed us back around her tub, where I could watch again the soapy bubbles and the delicate colours they made. Sometimes Bridgie gave us an enamel jug full of hot soapy water. Then we broke a bit of a stick off an elder branch in the grove, scooped a hollow in the middle to make a bubble stick, and stood it into the jug and blew until we had a jug full of bubbles. We sat on the warm grass and blew the bubbles into the air, watching them float away in their gorgeous, transparent colours and dissolve into nothingness. Fascinated by colours, on one occasion I watched intently a wasp which had landed on the edge of the tub, his bright yellow stripes contrasting vividly with the dark brown timber of the tub. Unfortunately, I was not satisfied merely to watch but put out my finger to test if the wasp was real and he proved in no uncertain terms that he was.

Blankets washed, Bridgie turned her attention to the other parts of the beds. On top of the wire spring came the horsehair mattress and the tick filled with feathers and down from the farm pluckings. Both the mattresses and the ticks she threw out of the bedroom windows or down the stairs and then she draped them across the hedges in the garden to give them "a good soak of sunshine". She rounded up my father to get him to help her stretch wire springs; such maintenance was vital as sagging springs were bad for the back and might slip off the iron frame of the bed pitching the unwary sleeper head downwards and legs in the air.

The padded and multi-coloured patchwork quilts awoke a poetry in Bridgie's soul. She washed them with soap and water blended with tender appreciation for the hours of concentration that had gone into their creation. But it was the heavy lace bedspreads that brought out the best in her. These were not for ordinary sleepers but were reserved for honeymoons, childbirth and death, for the grandeur of lace was appropriate to grace all of the most important occasions in life. Bridgie turned the washing of one of these special bedspreads into an act of reverence: running her fingers gently over the intricate design she would talk softly to this family heirloom. "What beauty! How many did you breed? How many did you born? How many did you bury? All life has passed beneath you from the beginning to the end." Washing the bedspread she became a different person as her face lit up and filled with joy.

She rinsed the bedspread and squeezed it gently and then took it to the little meadow below the house where she spread it out on the young grass and wild flowers. The rest of the washing she pegged on the wire clothesline or spread across the hedges, but the lace bedspread got special treatment. Finally she brought it in and folded it carefully, placing mothballs between its creases, and laid it, wrapped in tissue-paper, in the old trunk where my mother stored family treasures.

If the day's washing finished early Bridgie would draw buckets of warm soapy water from the wash-tub and scrub down the upstairs bedrooms. Then she emptied the timber tub onto the kitchen floor and scrubbed it out. From start to finish it was a heavy day's work but

ALWAYS ON A MONDAY

Bridgie was as full of bounce at the end as she had been at the beginning. She was never told what to do but worked at her own pace, treating our house and our washing as if they were her own.

When she had finished she had tea with my mother at the kitchen table where she aired all her family grievances. Her husband was in her opinion over-fond of his drink, and so she gave him "a few belts" when she felt that he needed her to "bate a bit of sense into him". But the one great regret in her life was that, although she had four daughters, she had no son. As she sat after her hard day's work, swirling her tea around in her cup and puffing her fag, she would say, "Four children, missus, but not one little tassle in my house". It was one of a number of her phrases which confused me on first hearing, and to my mother fell the task of explaining it.

One thing that never changed about Bridgie was her farewell to us children. As she went out the door she would call out to us, "I'll be back, brats, on Monday; always on a Monday".

Winter Journeys

THE MOST AWKWARD outdoor chores always seemed to arise on cold, snowy winter days, and few if any were more awkward than taking a turkey to the cock or a battery to town to be charged. The two batteries on which our large brown box radio relied bore little resemblance to their slimline descendants of today. For a start, one was dry, the other was wet and both were large and filled with acid. The radio itself sat on the base of the back window in the kitchen and, as the walls of the house were about three feet thick, the window-ledge had sufficient room for both the radio and, behind it, the two batteries, to which it was connected by leads with little brass claws that fitted under the black and red knobs on the tops of the batteries. Sometimes a green mould formed at the connection point and my father would scrape it away with his penknife until the claw was shining brass again. The dry battery lasted a long time but the wet one had to be charged more often, depending on how much the radio was used, and scarcely a day went by without one of us children being told, "Turn off the radio and don't be wasting the batteries".

One cold January day, after he had taken hay to the sheep down by the river, my father came in and, rubbing his hands together to improve the circulation, went straight to the radio, having as always arranged to finish his morning jobs in time to catch the news on either Radio Eireann or the BBC. But today Radio Eireann had been reduced by a fading battery to a whisper and the BBC was lost in the airwaves over the Irish sea. In summer batteries in need of recharging could be carried into town on the creamery cart, but in winter when the cows took their holidays the cart no longer made the journey, and so now I was dispatched to town.

Dressed in an extra layer of clothes I clutched the heavy glass battery with icy fingers. Some protection from the pressure of the handle was provided by a pair of furry mittens my godmother had sent from America, but nevertheless I shifted it frequently from one hand to the other to balance the wear and tear. Occasionally I rested, and where the snow was still on the ground I traced the bird- and rabbit-tracks that could be found along by the hedges. Animals that usually merged into the colours of the countryside now contrasted vividly with the snow, and my journey to town invariably took longer than necessary when there was so much along the way to sidetrack me.

Arriving in town I went straight to Jim's pub which, amongst its many other services, charged batteries. Midway in the long counter was a big brown cupboard where charging batteries fizzed and spluttered in harmony with the surrounding activities. Old men sat spitting and arguing around the fire, while on the high shelves bottles of amber liquid glinted richly in the firelight. If one of the customers recognized me I was called over and seated by the fire for a warm-up and treated to a glass of fizzy lemonade.

There was one old man, however, who had to be kept at a safe distance. He had earned the name "Catch" on account of his tendency to grab at any female form from eight to eighty years of age which came within striking distance. He was a small man who flopped around inside an enormous pair of wellingtons that came up over his knees. He lurched from periods of absolute silence to bouts of frenzied conversation but, apart from the occasional grab at a passing female, he was harmless.

I loved the smell of the porter and whiskey and most of all the mixed tobacco smells off the old men who chewed on a varied assortment of clay, straight and giant turn-down pipes. Sometimes one of the old men in a burst of alcoholic exuberance would get up and do a little dance, to be told by one of his good companions that he had "the makings of a great dancer" and by another that he should "sit down and have a grain of sense".

Finishing my lemonade and dodging "Catch", I collected a fully charged battery in exchange for my run-down one and set out for home. On a lucky day a neighbour might come along in a horse and cart piled with bags of meal and flour. Having climbed up the spokes of the wheels I would clamber in over the sideboard and nestle down comfortably between the bags in the middle of the cart, while the battery was wedged firmly against the sideboard in case it leaked.

The drive shortened the journey home but I always called a halt in front of Mrs Casey's because we children simply never came home from town without calling to see her. She warmed many a cold winter's evening with a big bowl of steaming-hot bread-and-butter pudding, but most of all she warmed it with her welcome. She coaxed her huge, long-haired sheepdog, Bran, back from the fire to make way for me to get into the corner inside the bellows where no draught could catch me. After the hot pudding she gave me sweet, strong tea and a boiled brown egg (she had no respect for white ones) from the red-combed hens which thronged her haggard.

Fortified by her goodness I arrived home with the dark and my father breathed freely again, saved from the awful prospect of a night without the radio.

The battery was carried to town by road, but taking the turkey to the cock was a cross-country marathon. Normally our turkey-cock made this journey unnecessary but one year the old boy decided that he needed a sabbatical. He paid a terrible price for his jaded sexual urges because my mother promptly pulled his neck and he became the following Sunday's dinner. This did not, however, solve the turkey-hen's problem: she wanted a turkey-cock and lay on the ground, wings fluffed out and neck stretched forward passively. "The turkey is lying," my mother said, and if our cock was in no condition to do the needful a couple of miles across the fields was one that could.

The turkey-hen was bundled into a coarse grey bag; the top was tied but a hole was made where she could put her head out for air, and my sister Clare and I set out with our captive companion. A live turkey in a bag makes an awkward parcel and we took it in turns to carry her under our arms. With one arm firmly around her she was manageable but sometimes her legs got in the way and she dug her long claws into us. As we were leaving home my mother had advised us to keep her head out of the hole in the bag in case she might be stifled. The problem was, however, that when the turkey stretched out her long neck she was quite capable of testing your cheek or finger for flavour. Although she did it out of curiosity rather than aggression, her motivation did nothing to soften the peck, so as soon as we had home and my mother at a safe distance we shut the turkey's door to the outside world.

As we crossed the fields we discussed the complex question of sex and turkeys. The ground was covered with hard, frozen snow and when we came to a hilly field we skated down the icy slope. Abandoning the turkey with her head newly liberated and poking out of the bag we climbed back up the hill and skated down again and again, but when it started to snow we collected our turkey and moved on, once more shutting her door.

Entering the gap of a small field beside the wood, we saw under the total whiteness of the snow-draped trees a cock pheasant resplendent in his colourful coat of rich, vivid feathers. He was magnificent in his gorgeous plumage with his elegant neck stretched out questioningly at our intrusion into his domain. Accompanying him were two less colourful hens and then another cock came out from behind a clump of snow-covered bushes quite near us. They filled the little field with their presence and we stood holding our breath for fear we might frighten them away. Then Clare had a brainwave.

"Do you think," she whispered, "that if we let the turkey out of the bag the cock pheasants would solve her problem?"

But before we could try out her theory there was a sudden flutter of wings and they all disappeared into the wood.

The greatest obstacle to be overcome on our journey was the river but luckily the water was low and we wobbled over large crossing stones having first flung the turkey across to the opposite bank, where she landed with a loud squawk. We came to the top of the last hill and looked back along the valley. There, under the trees, striding along at his leisure, was a big tawney fox. "That's the boy," said Clare, "that would solve all our turkey's problems." We pulled her head out through the hole in the bag and directed her gaze towards the fox, who looked enquiringly across the river at us and then trotted off into the wood.

Finally we reached our destination and Mrs Cleary

relieved us of our burden. As she saw to the turkey's needs we went into the warm kitchen where her daughter, who was about the same age as ourselves, gave us tea and buns she had just baked. As we had our tea Clare went to the back window of the kitchen, which overlooked the haggard, and gave us a running commentary on the turkey copulation outside. When Mrs Cleary was satisfied that all had been accomplished, our turkey was returned to us and we went home across the snow-covered fields, at a faster pace now as both the night and the snow were falling fast.

Capeen

BILL BROUGHT HIM late one winter's night, curled up asleep in his tweed cap. He was tiny: pure white with one black ear and a black stumpy tail, I had never seen a puppy so small. Reaching out a timid finger to test if he was real, I felt his downy puppy hair; then he opened one black eye flecked with gold and peered up at me. A tiny, petal-soft tongue curled around my finger. Then he stretched out full length in the comfort of Bill's cap but still he was not quite the length of it. Satisfied with his stretch, he sat up on his miniature hind legs and gave a cheeky little bark and I fell in love with him there and then. Bill handed him to me and he was mine, and I called him Capeen.

Numerous dogs rambled around the farmyard: greyhounds – five or six of them – and a couple of sheepdogs, and a black gun dog called Darkie who went fowling with my father. My mother had a golden rule that none of them were allowed in the house, but Capeen broke that rule on his very first night. He was too small, I maintained, to go outside, and anyway the big dogs might attack him. He slept that night in a box of hay by the fire, where he was to remain for many nights, but when the weather got warmer in the summer I transferred him to a spare manger in the stable.

He was a beautiful little dog who never grew very big, but what he lacked in size he made up for in intelligence.

He could do everything but talk, though in any case the two of us did not need conversation because we communicated perfectly without words. We went rambling together through the fields and he chased rabbits just for the fun of it because his legs were too short to catch them and even if he had he would have been more surprised than them. We had races up and down the meadows and when I buried him in hay he quickly burrowed out and cocked his perky little head sideways almost saying, "You can't fool me, I'm too smart".

When we children went swimming in the river Capeen came too and he loved coursing through the high rushes of the inches to dry himself after his swim. He ran home before us, his stubby black tail darting in and out around the thistles that grew in the wet fields by the river. He conveyed us towards school every morning but came no further than the crab-tree at the bottom of the first field, where he was waiting again every evening. In the mornings he looked sadly after us but in the evenings he went mad with delight at the sight of us. I scooped him up to hug him and he almost tore the hair off my head with his dancing paws and swept his moist tongue all over my face.

A great sense of adventure filled his heart and he loved investigating new places, which sometimes led him into corners from which he could not extricate himself. Once when peering curiously over the top of the deep lime-kiln he toppled in and my father had to put down the long hay-barn ladder to rescue him. On the way up the ladder my father scolded him for his stupidity but Capeen, who was always bubbling with fun, licked his face in thanksgiving and, as a final token of appreciation, knocked my father's cap off so that he had to go back down again to bring it up.

Capeen did not like the greyhounds and barked at them, teasing them to chase him; then he would run into some small corner which they could not fit into and from his safe bolt-hole he would growl out at them. Darkie, a gun dog trained to raise snipe and woodcock, was his friend and sometimes they went hunting together with my father. Capeen just went along for the fun of it but was smart enough to do exactly as he was told.

He and the cats waged continuous warfare; sometimes he chased them and sometimes they chased him, but one cat he never chased was old Minnie, because he had learnt the painful lesson that whenever she got her claws into action she would leave a mark. Some mornings he jumped into the creamery cart and went to the creamery with my father. He enjoyed the journey into town and sat imperiously on the setlock looking contemptuously down at the town dogs which snarled up at him. My father loved him because, as he said himself, he was "a real smart little fellow". But he was the bane of my mother's life and Bridgie threatened regularly to "bate sense into him", because his one great weakness was for washing which was flapping in the breeze; sheets waving above his head provided sweet temptation which he could never resist. He swung back and forth on the washing until Bridgie, who was ever on the look out for him, brought him down to earth with a fine hard slap across the tail. He would then scamper off and hide under a bush at the bottom of the garden with only his nose in view, while he waited until such time as he judged it safe to make a comeback.

He broke all the rules of the house and got away with it. Some cold nights I sneaked him upstairs and he slept at the foot of my bed. When I estimated that my mother was about to come to say goodnight I covered him with a pillow and, smart fellow that he was, he never gave the game away. When we sat at the table for meals on a long stool that seated a row of us, Capeen sometimes lined up with the rest of us. When Bridgie saw this she would roll her eyes to heaven and declare, "Glory be to God, where will I see that dog next? I know where I'll see him: kneeling on top of the altar-rails with his tongue out waiting to receive – there's nothing beyond that fellow. Ye should take him to school because he is wasting his time around here."

One summer evening no Capeen waited at the crab tree as I returned from school. We were puzzled but not unduly alarmed. It was a Monday, so he could have been under his bush doing penance; or he could have gone hunting with Darkie, as sometimes they went off on their own. However, on investigation we found that he was not under his bush and Darkie was lying by the front door, so after a hurried dinner we began to search the hay barn, the stables, the stalls, but there was no trace of him. We went out into the fields and called but no answering bark came. The search went on for hours and after the cows had been milked the adults joined in and even Bridgie, her bag apron wrapped around her head, helped in the search.

That night when I said the rosary I begged God to mind Capeen because I did not like the idea of him being alone in the dark wherever he was. I went to bed with a heavy heart but deep down hope still flickered. I tried not to cry because that would have been to give in and abandon hope, and that was too terrible to think about. But when I moved my leg under the spot where Capeen sometimes sneaked in to sleep it was hard to hold back the tears.

When I woke the next morning it took a few seconds for the previous evening's happenings to flood back to me. I jumped out of bed hoping to see that he was running around in the yard, but only Darkie was out there, sleeping in their usual corner. That day in school passed like a nightmare, and coming home that evening and arriving at the crab-tree to find no Capeen dancing in delight was worse. My father was waiting for me at the gate.

"We found him," he called, and for a second my heart was bursting with joy. "He's dead," he said simply. "He got caught under the gate in the bottom meadow and the gate must have slipped and killed him."

I could not believe it; it was just too much to take in. How could such a stupid thing have happened? There was a pain inside me and a hard lump in my throat and I squeezed my eyes to blink back the tears.

"Where is he?" I whispered.

"He's in his manger," Dad said.

He lay stretched out cold and rigid on the hay with blood at the corner of his mouth. My tears ran down on top of him.

That evening we dug his grave in the animal graveyard under the old apple-tree at the bottom of the orchard, and Darkie and Minnie came with us. I hated Darkie then because he was alive and Capeen was dead and I felt that in some way he should have looked after Capeen better. I blamed myself, too, for not having found him the night before when perhaps he had still been alive.

We lined a timber apple box with one of Bridgie's torn sheets and placed him in it; in death he seemed bigger than he had been alive. We eased his coffin down into the ground and covered him with soft brown earth. The apple-tree stood at the head of the grave with leafy arms outstretched in the shape of a cross. On its bark with hammer and chisel we carved his epitaph in letters as large as the trunk could accommodate: GOOD BYE CAPEEN.

If Ever A Man Suffered

LICENCES WERE REQUIRED for dogs, bulls and guns, yet my father's cut-throat razor was covered by no such permit and lay in a harmless-looking slim black box on top of the tall press in the kitchen. It had a six inch long, paper-thin blade that curved off at one end and hooked into a white bone handle at the other, and it folded back into this handle when not in use.

Every Sunday morning after breakfast my father reached up to the top of the high press, took down the black box and placed it on the ledge inside the window. The front window of our kitchen was set in a recess with a deep ledge running all around it, and this was the altar of his weekly shaving ritual. He transferred a black leather strap from the side of the press to a rusty hook beneath the window-ledge before demanding, "Where's my shaving mug?" It was always in the same place, on the top shelf of the press beside the big meat-dish, but it seemed he could never find it without being told. Inside the mug was shaving soap and a soft bristle brush in a bone base.

Having lined up his equipment on the ledge he lifted down a small mirror that hung beside the clock and asked, "Is that bloody kettle boiling yet?" The kettle was, of course, always boiling at this point in his preparations, but because he could never fill the shaving mug without the kettle spout overshooting the top of the mug and causing him to be blinded in a shower of ashes when the water hit the fire, my mother intervened and placed the mug of boiling water on the ledge with the rest of his accoutrements where it promptly fogged up the mirror.

"How the blazes can I shave when I can't even see my cursed face?" he said in eloquent thanks for her help.

Off came his cap and coat and, reduced to his striped shirt and waistcoat, he pulled a creaking *súgán* chair up in front of the window and commenced the operation. His cap hung off one corner of the back of the chair and over the other corner my mother placed a small towel. The biggest towel in the house she spread across his knees. He reached down for the leather strap and, finding himself too close to the window, he jolted the *súgán* backwards, knocking his cap onto the floor. He then stretched the strap to its full length and moistened it with a thumb dipped in the bowl of water; if the water was too hot he spat on the leather instead. When he judged the strap to be just right he opened the black box and unfolded the cut-throat. Catching it by its delicate, bone handle he lightly flicked it up and down the ebony strap; the silver blade of the razor gave a soft, swishing, sensuous hiss as it glinted in the morning light.

To judge whether the blade had reached the necessary sharpness he required a hair, with which his own head could not oblige him as he was completely bald. So I dangled in front of him a long, light hair which I had eased from the top of my head and he lanced it with the razor, which was then pronounced ready for action. He dipped the bristle brush into the mug of warm water and sloshed its dripping head across the shaving soap. When he had worked up a fine white lather he brushed it all over the lower half of his face. This gave him a benevolent, Santa-Claus appearance but there the similarity ended because this Santa was volcanic and started to erupt as soon as he applied the razor to his face.

The razor took on the character of a deadly enemy as it moved across his chin, bringing lather and hair before it and blood behind. He waved it in the air, viewed his ravaged visage in the foggy mirror and swore at it, "You bloody bastard, are you trying to kill me?" A battle of sorts ensued and as my father's temper worsened so the razor became blunter and the floor around him disappeared under dollops of white shaving lather streaked with blood and speckled with hair. The towel that my mother had hung on the back of his chair to absorb this residue was long forgotten. After each fresh onslaught he ran his fingers along the blade and swished the lather onto the floor. Gradually his face emerged, pink and tender with bloody nicks which he patched with bits of newspaper.

Shaving and first aid completed, he folded up his razor carefully and wrapped it in its faded yellow tissue-paper before returning it to its box. The performance was over for another week but the leading man had no intention of cleaning the stage. Retrieving his cap from the snowy floor he went upstairs to get ready for Mass, leaving that end of the kitchen in a chaos of shaving soap, water, towels and bits of discarded newspaper.

Once and once only my sister Clare and I were foolish enough to disrupt his shaving routine. It was the first Christmas at which we had a really good-sized Christmas tree and we had acquired tinsel for it from the Miss Bowlers' shop and stood it into the window recess in a butter box filled with stones. That Christmas morning, coming home from early Mass, we were met by a strange sight. My father was pinned against the window with the Christmas tree on his back and tinsel hanging off his ears. In shifting it out of his way to give himself room he had unsettled the tree's temporary rooting system, and in the middle of his shaving session it had tilted forward on top of him, balloons bursting and the Christmas fairy taking a nosedive from the top into his shaving mug. When we ran to his rescue we were met with a stream of language which was hardly in keeping with the season of goodwill.

"Take that hoor's melt of a Christmas tree off my back," he yelled.

We dragged the heavy, stone-filled box back and manoeuvered the tree into an upright position, thereby releasing him. But then we had to strip him of decorations which, in addition to tinsel, included a substance called angels' hair, which was meant to cover the tree in a shimmering glow but which was not to be touched once it was in position. And there and then we discovered why not. It had wrapped itself around my father to such an extent that the only way we could remove it was by unwinding it gently and methodically, but that proved impossible because he was dancing around the kitchen in a fit of jumping rage. Finally he tore upstairs, whipped off all his clothes and flung them down with instructions to "Get that bloody muck off them".

Whenever he recalled that episode afterwards he would raise his eyes to heaven and sigh, "If ever a man suffered".

Too Hot To Handle

EVERY SATURDAY EVENING the big old arm-chair just inside our parlour door was piled high with freshly washed clothes; not folded neatly but thrown there in big bundles which smelt of cool grass and fresh air. The clothes had been draped across bushes and hedges to dry, the sheets spread out on the green fields, and all came in smelling of wild flowers and the world outside, while some occasionally sported the evidence of a bird's blessing. By evening time the pyramid of clothes had reached the point of toppling over and my hour of reckoning had come.

I hated, abhorred and detested ironing. In our kitchen were two tables, one very large and the other of medium size; on this second table my mother baked and on Saturday it became the ironing-board. It was covered with an old, threadbare woollen blanket which was yellow with age, had three blue stripes at either end and was christened the ironing-blanket. Over it went two or three patched and holed sheets which had passed beyond further repair, and the aim was to get the holes of one to coincide with the sound parts of another.

The iron itself was hollow and made of iron with upright iron arms at both front and back which were bridged with a timber handle. Narrow at the front, it broadened towards the back where an opening was covered by a little door that slid up and down like a guillotine, and through this aperture heaters were slipped into the iron. These were the same shape as the iron and were made of pure, solid metal; they had been placed in the middle of the fire and left there until they had become so red hot that they were indistinguishable from the red sods of turf around them. It was torture to me to have to catch one of the heaters with long iron tongs and manoeuvre it into the opening in the iron. Any tilt in the wrong direction could have drastic consequences as I held the iron firmly in my left hand while the red-hot heater wobbled dangerously at the end of the tongs in my right.

Heater in and door closed, the iron was ready for action but at this point it was what my father aptly termed a "burning bastard". With no such thing as a control knob you could learn to match iron-heat to material only by trial and error. And what agonies I went through in those trials and errors! The ironing-sheets were the most immediate victims and quickly took on an auburn appearance. The tails of my father's shirts bore the evidence of many errors of judgement, for my mother always advocated testing the iron on shirt-tails first. Long, swallow-tailed and ample, the shirt-tails of the time were worn safely buried in the cavernous depths of trousers held up by braces. Even if one of the buttons which secured the braces popped, it was swiftly replaced by a nail, so there was never any chance of the shirt-tails making a public appearance and displaying iron-shaped scorches. Nevertheless, my father rained showers of curses on the offending iron whenever he was presented with yet another burnt offering.

The iron was a constant source of torment to me, and one of the problems it presented was that it could deposit soot and ashes on whatever you ironed if you did not take care when transferring the heater into it. A dirty iron placed on a damp, white table-cloth left an ashy or sooty mark buried deep in the fabric. Another common hazard was, of course, scorched fingers or wrists; the arms of the handle heated up as well, so the whole contraption radiated heat. As the heat of the iron cooled, seeming by this time to have transferred itself into my face and temper, it became comfortable enough to hold, but that meant that it was no longer warm enough to be effective so its companion was brought forth from the flames and the fiery agony was repeated.

Sheets, pillow-cases and table-cloths had all to be ironed, as well as everything we wore, so the ironing was no small job. Some of the dresses were starched, and the collars of the men's shirts were starched cardboard-stiff. If too dry, starched items were impossible to iron; if too wet, the iron clung to the damp starch. One of our neighbours, the redoubtable Mrs Casey, was an expert at starching and her husband's shirt-collar with its pristine white rigidity was always a source of wonder to me. Old Dan paid homage to this skill with a saying he had to describe a woman of exceptional efficiency: "Jakus me, she'd starch the tail of your shirt!"

The Burial Bonnet

NO ONE LOVED hardship like Bessie-Babe. She preferred other people's hardship but if none was available she could always be relied upon to come up with some of her own. The way Dan put it was that she had never heard of the resurrection because she had got stuck at the crucifixion, and she was the only person he knew who would have enjoyed the agony in the garden. She was an enthusiastic and appreciative attender at every funeral in the parish, and whenever we saw her wearing her special burial bonnet we knew that someone was either dead or on their last legs. Standing at the graveside she could turn on tears like a waterfall and for months afterwards if she met the mourners she liked nothing so much as to join them in a good cry. Indeed, she became a by-word in our house: if anyone cried over something and my father felt they were overdoing it he would say, "Don't be doing Bessie-Babe on it".

Once she fell seriously ill and it was agreed amongst the neighbours that hers could be the next funeral, but when another neighbour died the prospect of attending a funeral soon lifted her out of her sick-bed. As she stood at the graveside watching the coffin being lowered she remarked with a sob to Dan, who happened to be standing beside her, that she supposed she'd be next.

"That's what they're all saying anyway," he assured

her.

Bessie-Babe had a farm back the valley and sometimes Dan worked with her but declared that he could
not stay too long or he would die from hunger. She was
a widow woman and Dan firmly believed that she had
starved her husband to death.

"That woman," he would say, "was born in a grum-
bling month and is the manest woman who ever wore
shoe leather; as a matter of fact, she is the tightest and
most miserable strap under the canopy of heaven, and
that's a wide territory."

Another of Dan's pronouncements about her was
that she was "too clane to be dacent", and her house was
indeed spotless. "A place for everything and everything
in its place" was her motto, and whenever I was in her
house I was always afraid to sit down in case I would
upset something. She believed so strongly in keeping
everything in its place that she would not allow Dan
into her own kitchen but fed him in the scullery where
she kept her pots and pans. We were not sure whether
she did this out of an over-enthusiastic concern for
hygiene, which she certainly possessed, or notions of
grandeur. She undoubtedly considered herself a touch
smarter than the rest of us, and Mrs Casey used to say
of her, "That one has high ideas, like Taylor's gander
when he gets on top of the dunghill".

Always looking for bargains, she kept the shopkeepers in town on their toes. Indeed, if Ned wanted to
recommend something as representing great value he
would say, "Bessie-Babe bought this". She bought, in
fact, very little, being a devotee of patching patches and
darning darns. She took large baskets of eggs into town
where she bargained with the shopkeepers to get the
best possible price for them. If she succeeded in extract-
ing a high price then she would buy the neighbours' eggs
at the old, lower price and resell them to the shop.

Rabbits could also be sold to shops, and young fellows would often be seen cycling into town with rows of them hanging off the crossbars of their bikes. The rabbits provided them with good pocket-money but Bessie-Babe moved in on their territory for if there was money to be made she wanted to be in on it, and she became the only woman around who dealt in rabbits.

Every conversation with her opened with the same words: "Whisper here a minute", and then she would deliver herself of an endless litany of complaints. My father dreaded an encounter with her and would run a mile to avoid it; he used to say that she put years on him. One day, after having been cornered by her for a long session, he came in home and threw himself into the chair, quite exhausted.

"That woman," he declared, "is like a waxy hen's shit: there's no getting rid of her, she just clings on."

At a ripe old age she finally died and, having enjoyed burying so many, it was only right that she had a huge funeral herself. Dan was there, of course, and delivered the opinion that her burial bonnet should have been placed on top of her coffin like a soldier's cap.

Anyone For Pandy?

MY MOTHER BOILED a big, black pot of potatoes for the dinner every day except Sunday. Whether there were to be ten or twenty for the dinner, the same big pot was hung over the fire; the dangling pot-hangers were threaded through its ears while flames licked around its black bottom. A tin bucketful of purple potatoes was then poured in, thumping off the bottom and sides before being packed down under the iron cover. These spuds came straight from the bosom of mother earth and there was no need to limit the supply as there were plenty more where they came from. Another reason why so many went into the pot was because hungry spud-consumers came in five successive categories: human beings, cats, dogs, fowl and pigs. We, as befitted the supposedly most civilized of the five species, got the first bite.

The flowery spuds were judged ready for removal when they started to smile across the top of the pot. A huge ware dish, reminiscent of a feast Henry VIII might have held, was then placed in the centre of the kitchen table and potatoes were poured into it until there was a mountain of them. Smaller, younger members of the household facing each other across the table had to wait for the mountain to be demolished before they could gain sight of each other again. As the potato mountain diminished small hills of skins arose, until all were satisfied.

Jacket potatoes were the order of the day, but occasionally the luxury of pandy came our way. You were not judged worthy of pandy unless you were very young, very ill or "feeling delicate", as my father termed the state of being out of harmony with the world. Today pandy might be called mashed potato by the unenlightened, but it was not quite the same thing.

Pandy first required a big, soft, flowery spud with a long smile across its face. Starting at the smile, the skin was eased off gently and the naked spud, almost too hot to handle, was transferred fast by hand into another plate, leaving its clothes in a heap behind it. Next a lump of yellow butter was placed on top, from where it ran in little yellow streams down the sides. A gentle little poke with the fork opened up a cavity into which went a drop of milk or a spoon of cream skimmed off the top of the bucket, followed by a shake of salt. Finally, the entire slushy combination was lightly whipped together and frequently tasted to ascertain that the correct balance was being achieved. It took great care and a discerning palate to make really good pandy; it had to be yellow, soft, delicately flavoured, and as light as thistledown on the tongue. When you were sick or not feeling happy you judged how much your mother and the world loved you by the quality of her pandy. It was our antibiotic, our tranquilizer and our sleeping potion.

The royal spud ruled in the kitchen, but the king was also democratic, for he came down a step from the kitchen table into the dogs' bucket, where he was joined by surplus cabbage and turnips – the regular vegetables on our unvaried menu – and bits of bacon which were too fat or grizzly for us to eat. The various leftovers were hand-mixed to a gooey mess with the aid of vegetable water and fed in disused churn covers or rusty pans to a motley collection of cats and dogs. The dogs got the first round, starting with the biggest because all dogs, like most humans, believe in the survival of the fittest. When the little dogs had finished the cats came into their own, daintily licking around the edges and picking up delicate morsels that the slashing dogs' tongues had missed. Any leftover pandy was saved for the cats as they were considered discerning enough in their tastes to appreciate it. The pandy was placed in a saucer and surrounded by a river of milk, so the cats had eating and drinking in it.

The fowl tucked in next and the leftover potatoes with their jackets still on them were hand-mashed, oozing stickily between bruising fingers which crushed them out through their skins. This was then mixed with crushed oats and produced a grainy, substantial meal which the hens gobbled down appreciatively. The remaining pandy was reserved for the chickens whose taste-buds and beaks had not yet been coarsened by the pickings of the great outdoors; they pecked timidly at the fluffy pandy, its delicate consistency ideal for their baby stomachs. The tiny young chicks and the pandy blended together in a soft yellow colour combination.

Pigs provided the final destination of the potatoes. In the centre of their house was a circular iron trough, its base curled up saucer-like, with iron dividers to keep hungry heads apart and prevent bad manners in the trough. All surviving leftovers from the kitchen table were indiscriminately dumped in here, where they were wolfed down with total disregard for either flavour or finesse. Pigs were certainly not numbered amongst the connoisseurs of pandy, which provided comfort and sustenance to delicate humans, cats and, especially, the females of the species.

Molly's Cottage

ON TUESDAY EVENINGS we cleaned the eggs with damp cloths and bread soda, and the following morning we took a big basket of them down to Molly's, because Wednesday was the day the egg-lorry came to her cottage. I always looked forward avidly to what was for me one of the highlights of the week: the visit to Molly's cottage.

There was no gate between the road and her garden, only a gap in the mossy ditch which in the spring was covered with daffodils and in the summer was smothered with buttercups. Despite her goat's best efforts to devour everything in sight, Molly's flowers tumbled and climbed over the low stony ditch that surrounded her cobbled yard. The orange shafts of her donkey cart in the open shed contrasted with the black rick of turf. Often there was a bicycle or two in the shed which had been left by neighbours because behind Molly's cottage was a hill road which was easier to walk up without the encumbrance of a bike.

When we visited her on Wednesday mornings I always ran ahead as soon as her thatched roof came into view in order to get a few extra minutes to peer in over her half-door. The stillness of the shadowy kitchen reached out to me over the half-door and never failed to intrigue me. At first I could see nothing but the glow of the turf fire; I could smell the fire's peaty fragrance, and

I could hear the ticking of her clock and the clicking of her knitting needles. But gradually my eyes adjusted to the dimness and the dark objects inside came into focus.

Directly opposite the door her dresser displayed all Molly's ware, and I was familiar with every item. Blue saucers stood proudly on the top shelf, matching bread-plates beneath, and cups hung off the hooks on the edge of each shelf. Below them were her dinner plates and, at the base, her big meat-dishes. At the corner of one of the shelves was a special set of ware which she never used. Her mother had given it to her as a wedding present, having received it from her own mother. The cups were paper-thin china with pale pink roses and the whole set was Molly's pride and joy. It was seldom taken down but sometimes she allowed me to hold a cup just to feel how delicate and beautiful it was. In the open section at the bottom were stacked her kettles and pots.

She had a wonderful pair of hands that embroidered, knitted and sewed, but most beautiful of all was her lace. It covered a little table under the small, deep-set window and on the table was a brass lamp, her spare glasses, and whatever she happened to be working on at the time. The shelf over the fire which she called the "clevy" had a lace runner over an edged oilcloth; a pair of glass dogs sat there beside her clock, in front of which I used to sit waiting for its lovely, mellow chime. Every chair in the room was softened with plump feather cushions in embroidered and lace covers.

Much of her time she spent sitting beside her glowing turf fire, always busy with her hands, the clicking of needles often the only sound apart from the ticking of the clock and the clucking of the hens outside. A knitted shawl curved around her shoulders, and over her long, black, satin skirt a white, lace-edged apron rested when she was sewing. Peeping from beneath her long skirt her kid-leather shoes glinted in the firelight; a small, dainty figure, she seemed almost like a doll and was the first adult whom I was tall enough to look down on.

She was always delighted to see us and when she wrapped her arms around us in welcome she was as soft as a ball of her own knitting wool and smelt of lavender. As soon as she had us seated by the fire she hung the kettle over it; nobody ever called to her without getting a cup of tea coloured with rich goat's milk and a slice of the delicious cream-cake which she baked in a very small bastable.

Molly was the same age as my grandmother but I never thought of her as old, only as kind and rather frail. Her face was wrinkled with smiles and her brown eyes twinkled with humour. The biggest treat she could give me was to let me into her bedroom where her lacemaking really came into its own, edging the pillow-cases and draping down over the bed in the most gorgeous bedspread. Her dressing-table, chest of drawers and window-sill all had lace cloths, and on a whatnot in the corner lace cloths peeped over the edge of the little shelves on which family photographs stood in silver frames. Beside the bedroom fireplace was a clock with weights and chains and if the weights were far enough down she would allow me to pull the chains.

It was an entirely feminine house lacking any trace of male influence. As a young girl Molly had spent many years in America where she had married a man "with wanderlust in his legs", as she said herself. When she had returned to the home cottage he had stayed there with her for a few months but soon became restless and set off on his travels again, coming and going several times but never remaining long. And then one day she had received a telegram informing her that he had been killed in an accident. She brought him home and buried him in the graveyard overlooking the river. One day she gave me a present of a little white china jug with a gold rim, saying, "Pray that my wanderer is at peace". I took her at her word: I called it my praying jug and kept holy water in it.

I often thought that heaven could well be Molly's cottage on a larger scale. One evening my father called to visit her and found her asleep in her chair, as it seemed; Molly had left her cottage and had gone, undoubtedly, to the real heaven. When next I entered the house, for once I did not pause at the half-door but went instead directly through the kitchen to her bedroom where she had been laid out in her lovely bed of lace with her crochet shawl around her shoulders. All her clocks had stopped and I thought that my heart would break, knowing that I would never again sit with her waiting for them to chime.

The Second Step

I LEFT THE OLD stone school across the fields and moved on to the local secondary school in the nearby town; I left my childhood behind and stepped into adolescence. My new school was three miles from the main road entrance to our farm, and our house was almost another half-mile back from the road. Every morning we walked to school, leaving the house at about half past eight, and every evening we started the return journey at about four, arriving home at around five. In the half-light of winter mornings we dragged ourselves out of bed and gathered together some kind of packed lunch while eating our breakfast. There was no question of my mother preparing lunches as she was already out milking the cows, so self reliance came early to us.

I was definitely not a morning person and it took the three and more miles into school to bring me gradually into touch with the world around me. As we walked down the road we drove the cows of one of the neighbouring farmers back to the fields after milking. When we reached a field further down the road they turned in at a gap, and sometimes I was so far removed from reality that I drifted in amongst them. Occasionally a slash of a tail across my face shocked me into sudden wakefulness and I came to my senses only to find that I was wedged between two large, round-bellied cows and it would take a good thump on the rump of one of them to open the trap I had entered.

Horses and carts with tall milk churns trundled by and sometimes, if we were few in number, might give us a spin. If we got a lift on a cold winter's morning we could warm ourselves then against the warm milk churns, standing between them or sitting on top. If, however, the cart jolted going over a stone or because the horse suddenly quickened at a slap of the reins, this could bring a spray of milk out from under the churn covers, resulting in a warm footbath. Or, if you were sitting in comfort on a piece of hay or a coarse bag on the setlock, you could enjoy the doubtful privilege of receiving this shower of milk down the back of your neck. By evening, in summer at least, the milk would have dried to a tacky and uncomfortable consistency and would be exuding a strong sour smell, causing others to do their best to avoid you.

When there was a pig market in town we drove the pigs before us on our way to school. But on arrival at the edge of the town we abandoned them to the adult in charge as we felt it beneath our dignity to be seen chasing pigs along the streets. Thick-skinned, stubborn animals, the pigs often created chaos by paying unwelcome visits through open shop-doors. Their baby bonhams were brought to market in a pony crib where they squealed in protest when jobbers poked amongst them testing their potential for developing into grade A bacon. The pig market filled the early morning air of the town with grunts and squeals and perfumed it with pungent farmyard smells. As the bonhams were confined to cribs and the sows were usually restrained by reins, only a small number of pigs actually ran around disrupting the normal life of the town, but even these few could make a mighty contribution to the general mayhem.

The fair days when calves and cows poured into the

town created real havoc. On our way to school we would meet jobbers out on the road waiting to catch an unwary farmer and secure a bargain. These jobbers, wily operators who were well versed in the skills of bargaining and who moved from fair to fair trading livestock, were different in their appearance from farmers; they always seemed to wear fawn overcoats and brown leather boots, they generally had slick, suave appearances, and they were smooth talkers. Bargaining could go on all day with much toing and froing, and often a middle-man called a tangler clinched the deal and took his own reward from it.

I would watch the varieties of men at the fair as they struck the poses that seemed an essential part of their business, never quite getting used to their habit of spitting onto their hand before offering it for the final handshake to seal their agreement. Despite all the spitting and handshakes, arguments about luck money usually ensued; the man who had sold was expected to return some token amount to the buyer to give him luck with the animal, but this luck money could often be the cause of another protracted argument. The entire bargaining session, which often lasted many hours, was an exercise in debating skill, oratory and one-upmanship, all occasioned by the simple necessity of selling a cow. The grand finale of the whole performance could take place in the middle of an admiring circle of onlookers, all of whom felt free to voice their own opinions on the deal. Sometimes hidden within the ranks of the onlookers might be a "puffer", whose function it was to raise the price despite having no intention of buying.

The best of all the fairs was the horse fair which took place only twice a year, in spring and autumn, and at which the amounts of money involved were much greater. Most farmers had two horses, and sometimes a pony for doing handy jobs like going to the creamery; donkeys, too, were very plentiful. All the farmers from the surrounding countryside came into town and were joined there by hordes of tinkers from all over the country who brought colour and excitement with them. Often, after many hours of drinking, they would finish off the day with a big fight, either between themselves or by taking on a few locals who were brave enough or, more likely, drunk enough to get involved. Sometimes a fight that had started between a tinker man and his wife could gather momentum and participants as it went on, and then the women would be likely to turn and throw in their lot with their menfolk. Sometimes, too, those who had started as opponents could join forces against locals who had perhaps gone to the assistance of one of them who had seemed to be losing the battle.

All in all the horse fair was an occasion of much commotion in the town when hard bargaining and great drinking combined as old friends put the world to rights over big, frothy pints. Sawdust and straw was thrown on the pub floors to absorb the muck coming in on the farmers' boots. At one of these fairs my father met an old friend down from the hills and they went for a pint where the old man smoked a pipe and spat continuously into the sawdust. The lady of the house was fussier than most and viewed old Jack with growing contempt until finally she brought from behind the counter a large spittoon, an item designed for such occasions and the likes of Jack. But Jack had never before seen a spittoon, and so ignored it completely and continued to spit on the floor, though she moved it around many times trying to place it in the most strategic position to serve its purpose. Finally old Jack, in a fit of annoyance at her antics, shouted at her, "Woman, if you don't take that blasted thing out of my way I'll spit into it!"

At the end of the town was Kate Brady's doss-house, where anybody who had no bed to go to, or who was unable to make it back to his home, found refuge. Kate had one enormous room with a wooden floor free of the clutter of furniture. She had a stick of white chalk with which she drew out each person's allotment, and she maintained law and order with a blackthorn crop. On a quiet night sleeping space was ample and guests could stretch out in comfort, but when times were busy things tightened up as the night progressed.

Our journey to and from the local secondary school helped us absorb many aspects of the life of the town. The school had been set up by a young graduate whose father had taught in our old national school in the fields. He and his wife and sister rented an old house and two rooms in a local hall. These two buildings – their house and the school – were around the corner from each other and there was much running back and forth past the Catholic church, which stood on the corner. Usually we had about four teachers and our number must have been around a hundred, so we all knew each other pretty well.

Academic achievement was not high on our list of priorities and, though the teachers applied as much pressure as they thought necessary, I never regarded exams as something to get excited about. For some strange reason I enjoyed doing them and felt that I could always do better when there was just the challenge of the paper and myself. My father was not greatly interested in examination results, and that took pressure off us. There was one boy in our class who had a father who was very anxious that he do well and I felt quite sympathetic towards him as not only had he the exam to contend with but a father looking over his shoulder as well.

We covered all the usual subjects, but Latin and Maths were my two heartbreakers. "Mensa" and "agricola" had no magic for me and I got thoroughly fed up translating Virgil back and forth. As for algebra and the mystery of how A plus B equalled C, it was like the Blessed Trinity to me and beyond human comprehension. I came to the conclusion that when God had created my brain he had omitted the mathematical department, and the only interest I ever had in Einstein was when I heard that he, too, had found school difficult. True or not, it at least brought a human dimension to him.

English was my special love and I was fortunate enough to have a teacher blessed with both brilliance and impatience; her love of English and her striving for perfection triggered her annoyance at the struggle she encountered in trying to drag us to some kind of literary heights. She put everything she possessed into teaching, but it was not until years later that any of us appreciated her efforts.

Christian Doctrine was the subject of a novel approach, in which one teacher brought a dozen songbooks into class and for half an hour every day we raised the roof with a mixture of rebel songs and hymns. Whatever about the religious content of the class we certainly associated it with zest and enjoyment.

Our school being so convenient to the church, we were roped in to contribute long Latin chants whenever there was a High Mass for the dead. We made an enthusiastic group of mourners in our enjoyment at the thought of the classes we were missing. On 2 November we did rounds for the Holy Souls, a custom which consisted of going into the church, saying a prescribed number of prayers, coming out and going back in again to repeat the performance. Our religious fervour increased as lunch-hour extended into school-time, and we hailed souls out of purgatory by the dozen. My father was always very sceptical about these rounds: when I came home from school and announced to him that I had so many rounds under my belt, he would give a wry smile at what he called "the whole crazy carry-on".

However, I had great faith in the power of novenas and prayer, and exam time was when I sought divine intervention most intensely. I had a novena for each subject, and St Patrick was the man in charge of Latin; someone had informed me that he had found Latin very difficult and had promised to help anyone with similar difficulties. My prayers were not motivated by any ambition to become a Latin scholar, but the idea of a silent army of saints waiting to be called into action appealed greatly to me. So, St Patrick was appointed Dean of Languages and in the event he came up trumps.

"Alice Taylor," my teacher asked, "how did you get honours in Latin? There must be some mistake."

But there was no mistake and it did not surprise me one bit, because my mother had always believed that prayer could move mountains, not to mind conquering Virgil.

The supervisor for our Inter Cert exam, which was conducted in the local dance-hall, was an old dragon who had me terrified but who failed to intimidate one of the boys sitting next to me. As the exam progressed he constantly checked his facts from a book which he drew from inside his coat. When I challenged him outside about the risk he was taking he just laughed and said, "Sure, I didn't give a damn whether she caught me or not".

The last subject in the exam was drawing from natural form. A more lenient supervisor would have told us the subject matter beforehand, but our dragon remained tight-lipped. She had reckoned, however, without the resourcefulness of my cool copying friend. He went into the garage underneath the hall and persuaded one of the mechanics to reverse a car under the trap-door in the floor. Standing on top of the car he was able to get into the hall through the trap-door and he reappeared moments later with the news that a wall-flower standing in a vase was all set up for the next sitting. At that stage the knowledge was unlikely to benefit us but we did feel a delightful sense of victory over our rigid lady supervisor.

Half-way through my secondary education a new school was acquired when an old Church of Ireland church became available. This was divided up into classrooms and for the first time we were all accommodated under one roof. Here the partition walls reached a height of only about twelve feet – far short of the ceiling – so the hum from the other classes could be heard in each classroom; we were able to gauge the tempers of all the teachers from the tones coming over the partition. Oak rafters arched high above our heads and sunken windows in thick, ancient walls gave the church a special atmosphere. Our nearest neighbours were the Protestants, including Sarah Curran, who had worshipped here and who now rested eternally beneath the trees beside the church. While they might have regarded learning as a suitable replacement for praying, they must surely have turned in their graves at the din created by scores of boisterous youngsters now stampeding around their once quiet and hallowed corner.

For five years we walked the hilly road into secondary school, carrying our books in sacks on our backs or by hand in cases, and we got to know the people in the houses along the way. In the main street of the town was a little bakery where fresh doughnuts were baked every Thursday and the smell, which met us as we came down the street, set our mouths watering. Later, on a winter's evening we might sink our teeth into warm sugary doughnuts, and the eating of them shortened our journey.

When we arrived home one of us would dish up the

dinner my mother had left warming by the fire and another would light the tilly heater to heat the large upstairs bedroom set aside for study. After dinner we tidied up and lit the tall tilly lamp which stood on the dressing-table in the study bedroom. In the light from the lamp the brass knobs of the two iron beds glinted in the corner of the room. The table at which we laboured wobbled and groaned with books, and often its wood-worm tracks developed many and varied expressions as idle pencils investigated hidden tunnels rather than explore the books on its surface.

We studied here until supper-time at about seven o'clock, taking it in turns to go down and set the table and have things ready for the adults when they came in from milking the cows. And then, for the first time in the day, we all came together and discussed over supper the day's happenings. Afterwards we returned upstairs, though occasionally a good programme on the radio might draw our attention, and usually we finished our day at about ten o'clock when we came downstairs for cocoa and a chat. The rovers, as we called visiting neighbours, would be sitting around the fire, from which my father was often missing, having himself gone roving to another house. Soon, however, everyone returned to their own homes and then my mother got us all on our knees for the rosary.

Quench The Lamp

T HE PACE OF life was slow for those who grew up with oil lamps and candles. It was not advisable to go rushing around in candle-light as the way forward was not brightly lit and you could easily bump into various shadowy objects which would suddenly bring you to a painful standstill. Candle-light was kind, however, to ageing faces, cobwebs and bad housekeeping, its soft, flickering glow casting gentle shadows over many a blemish, human and otherwise. Old Tom, one of our neighbours, always advised against buying a horse or choosing a wife in candle-light, for they were the two principal occasions in life on which he felt you needed the harsh reality of daylight to guide you.

He never chose a wife himself and his reason for not doing so was a trifle unusual. Females, he said, were either Sunday girls or Monday girls. Sunday girls looked good but Monday girls were good, and the bonus in life was to get a Monday girl who looked like a Sunday girl. He never succeeded himself so he remained a batchelor, and because he was of my father's generation he declared that the tide had now gone out for him. He was an only son with seven sisters so the female of the species held no mystery for him. All his sisters had long gone from his home and he came visiting to our house most nights. Tom liked female company and perhaps our house, with so many girls in it, reminded him of his childhood.

As we grew older we began to be trusted with candles in our rooms and we fastened them to the iron bed-heads with pools of hot candle-grease. One of the greatest disadvantages of candles was the candle-grease that inevitably flowed freely onto everything in the house but mostly onto floors. Once a week we young ones were dispatched upstairs with blunt knives to scrape the candle-grease off the bedroom floors. It was a tedious job but for some strange reason it did not make us any more careful not to spill grease back on the same floors the following week. Maybe we were slow learners.

Often we read late into the night by candle-light, which bathed the bed in a soft yellow light and left the rest of the room full of flickering shadows. One night my sister Clare fell asleep with the candle alight on her bedside table, to be awakened hours later by the heat of a blaze beside her. She quenched the leaping flames quickly by smothering them in the heavy quilt off her bed, and luckily the result was nothing more serious than a burnt-up table-top and a scorched foot caused when she stepped on a red-hot scissors that had fallen through the table.

My father was never told about such calamities, because any such news would trigger off such a litany of his crucifixions that it was simpler and more desirable to keep him in the dark. How he and his easy-going wife had finished up with five daughters hell-bent on cracking his nerves was one of the mysteries of life which he would often ponder. If reincarnation had been on his list of beliefs and if choice had been involved, there were days on which he would gladly have opted for the life of a monk, the more silent and enclosed the order and the more distant from us the better.

As dusk gathered into the kitchen on a winter's evening, we would ask mother, "Is it time to light the lamp yet?" Earlier in the day the globe of the lamp had been washed with lukewarm soapy water and polished with a soft cloth or newspaper. The base had been filled with paraffin oil and the wick had been trimmed. All was done in readiness for the night because leaving these jobs till the natural light had gone could lead to breakages in the dusk, to overflowing oil and to frayed tempers as a consequence. The top of the wick, which had been burned black the night before, was trimmed off with a sharp scissors, and if the wick had burned out the new one had to have time to soak up the oil before being lit. Sometimes it was put down into the bowl of the lamp on the last night of the old wick. The paraffin oil itself was brought regularly in an oil can from town, and if it was forgotten the neighbours could always be depended on to come to the rescue.

At first the wick was kept down low after lighting to give the globe a chance to warm slowly, because sudden heat could crack it. A hairpin was sometimes hung on top of the globe to prevent this happening. Gradually the wick could be turned up, changing the soft yellow to a white glow, and then the shade was put on, softening the glow and diffusing the light evenly around the room from its position in an iron basket attached to the wall. When the large open fire was built up with logs and turf its leaping flames added to the lamp-light. Before going to bed, if some of her household were still abroad, my mother turned the lamp down low and left it to provide a soft welcome home to the latecomer.

A second oil lamp was kept in the parlour, and this was a rich relation of the kitchen model. It had a heavy, cream-coloured glass bowl embossed with green and pink flowers, and an elegant brass stand. The pink colour of the lampshade matched the base and was delicately fluted around the top in a way that always made me think of a ballerina doing a head-stand.

When the lamp was lit it bathed our parlour in a muted pink light, warming up the old bog-oak sideboard with its varied assortment of family treasures on top, including the gramophone. The dark marble fireplace shone in the lamp-light, which was reflected in the mirror above the mantelpiece. On either side of the mirror stood two ebony, semi-nude male figures which had been brought back from foreign parts by someone in an earlier generation of our family. My mother was not particularly partial to displaying semi-nude males in her parlour, but their antiquity gave them a metaphorical clothing of respectability and so she tolerated their presence. On the mantelpiece, too, were a little silver lady's shoe and two pink-and-white china ones.

The floorboards in the parlour were polished around a central square of lino decorated with roses, which was almost obscured by an enormous oak table which matched the sideboard. The walls were distempered in a pale pink colour and white, lace curtains hung from a long pole over the single window. The curtains were mostly for decorative purposes as you could see in through them if you so desired, and the cream, tasselled blind that hung in the recess of the window was seldom drawn. The table dominated the room and was surrounded by curved-back chairs with black leather seats. On the end wall, opposite the fireplace, hung a painting of my paternal grandmother, a smiling-faced woman with bobbed white hair who looked down on us with smiling eyes from a serenely beautiful face. A portrait of her husband, a tall, stern-looking bearded gentleman, hung on the wall beside the window, while a painting of my parents on their wedding day hung over the sideboard. Beside the fireplace and sunk into the deep wall was my mother's ware press, from which I often stole lump sugar, the presence of which was supposed to be known to her alone.

Between the press and the fireplace stood the rocking-chair: comfortable and ample, it was my idea of heaven to cuddle up in its many feather cushions, rocking back and forth, watching the fire casting shadows along the ceiling. I always felt that the pictures on the walls came alive then and no matter where I hid in the room my father's eyes seemed to follow me, for even on his wedding day he had apparently been alert for impending disaster. But my favourite picture was the one of my grandmother, who seemed to smile kindly on me. When I asked my father once how such a calm-looking woman had had such a temperamental son, he smiled and said, "The balance of nature: don't ever marry somebody of the same temperament as yourself – the blend of opposites is a better combination." I concluded from that that he took after his father. A great admirer of fine trees, fine horses and fine-looking women, he was inclined to be blunt. Once when a neighbour married a very plain-looking man my father sighed and said, "My God, they'll have to put all their daughters under the table".

The parlour was used for the Stations and visitors, and I loved it when the fire was lit there, awaiting family gatherings of one kind and another. When my older sisters left home and brought back friends to stay, they ate in the parlour and I always acted as parlour-maid because then I could listen in to fascinating grown-up conversations about boyfriends and falling in love. Until then I had only come across such things in books, but in the parlour I encountered them in real life, though at second hand. When my sisters graduated to bringing home boyfriends it was better again because then I could enjoy a close-up view of the real thing. The parlour was thus my first step towards the world outside or, rather, it was when the world outside began to come in under my curious gaze.

Having lived with the candle and the oil lamp for so long, we experienced the tilly lamp as a big breakthrough into a world of light in about 1950. It was a simple invention, still fed on oil but with a mantle replacing the wick and giving a much stronger light. It worked on the same principle as the gas lamps used now for camping, but with oil instead of gas as the source of power. Hot on the heels of the tilly lamp came the tilly heater, which brought warmth to rooms without fireplaces, a function that had previously been performed by cumbersome, evil-smelling oil heaters. For most of my secondary-school days my studying was done by the light of a tilly lamp in an upstairs bedroom heated by a tilly heater. Only necessities were catered for, and it was not deemed necessary to get a tilly lamp for the parlour, where bright light was less important.

Soon after the advent of the tilly lamp to our home canvassing started for the Shannon Scheme, which was to bring about a much greater change in our lives. This rural electrification scheme had to be canvassed for because, strange as it may seem now, some people were reluctant to accept electricity into their homes. One of our neighbours hesitated to take it, but when he discovered that we could not get it unless he did he decided to give his approval rather than inconvenience us. Another old friend absolutely refused despite all kinds of persuasions, declaring that it could not be safe to boil a kettle from a hole in the wall.

Teams of men went all over the countryside, digging holes for ESB poles which were dragged into position by horses. Electrical contractors came and helped people plan their house lighting, but it was all so new and difficult to get accustomed to that most people did not put in sufficient sockets. The light switches and sockets, a far cry from the sleek models of today, stood out on walls like ugly brown warts. Wires were not tucked away inside walls and above ceilings but could be traced all over the house as they crept around skirting boards like raised varicose veins, drawing their power from the heart of the big black meter above the kitchen door. Even before the power was connected I was afraid that if I touched anything electrical I might drop down stone dead.

Many were cautious, too, about the way in which they installed and used the unfamilar electricity. One man installed just one light on the upstairs landing of his house and told all his children to leave their doors open so that the light could shine in. When my father suggested to him that it would be bad for their eyes if they wanted to read in bed, he was told that they went to bed to go to sleep, not to read. Cost-cutting influenced people's approach to installation. One thrifty individual, with a view to cutting down on initial expenses, installed just one light-switch, so that when he turned this on the whole house lit up like a Christmas tree.

One of the things which electricity did away with was the primus, a little gadget fuelled by paraffin oil and lit by methylated spirits, which had to be kept clean with a primus needle to prevent it from shooting into yellow flames and sending smelly smoke signals all around the kitchen. The electric kettle was a great improvement and was the first electrical item to enter most houses, bringing the ease of a quick cup of tea without first having to light the fire or the primus. In its early years it was not, however, plugged in freely as that would have been considered the height of extravagance. A toaster soon followed the kettle into our house as my mother was always partial to toast. There were no pop-up toasters then, and the early days of electricity in our house were flavoured by the smell of burnt toast filling the kitchen and a fog of smoke billowing out from the toaster.

The concept of labour-saving devices such as washing-machines and fridges was too strange for us to swallow quickly. The one luxury my father did indulge in was a mains radio, and he was delighted not to be at the mercy of run-down batteries, but he refused to buy an electric razor and still used his old cut-throat monster. However, first we had to get accustomed to the bright light that flooded the entire house, and one thing to be said in its favour was that it made the journey upstairs to bed much less frightening; it was now no longer necessary to check under beds for lurking spooks or to peer through shadowy doorways for silent figures waiting to pounce. The magic of touching a switch and the whole room filling with instant light was thrilling for the first few weeks, and I went up and down stairs for no reason other than to experience the joy of turning on lights. Nevertheless, there was no question of lights being left on when nobody was in the room, because my father had a new headache, the electricity bill, and soon we were constantly being reminded that he had no shares in the ESB.

Out in the farmyard the electricity lit up the old cobweb-draped rafters of the stables and stalls and threw light on gynaecological interventions during calving time. It extended the working day, for jobs that had previously had to be completed before darkness fell could now be continued under artificial light. And although it made our working day longer it also made our lives easier in many ways. One thing was certain: it had changed our lives and changed them utterly, carrying us into a new world and leaving the old one behind.

The Gladioli Man

BEING THE YOUNGEST of five sisters had its disadvantages because it meant obeying many mistresses: they were all chiefs and I was the only Indian. As a consequence I spent more time and energy trying to avoid carrying out the instructions of older sisters than actually doing as I was told. My mother never dished out jobs because she worked on the principle that everything got done eventually: that when we got tired of looking at unwashed ware on the table we would get around to washing it; and that as we were sleeping in the beds it was up to us to make them, and to tidy our rooms. Never lecturing or nagging, she just left things undone while my older sisters took over and delegated household duties down along the line.

The weekly rota of jobs varied but one to which I strongly objected was the daily brushing of the upstairs floors and stairs. In performing this hated job I took regular rest periods and sat into a window-seat of one of the rooms to read a book, but when the sound of my busy footsteps ceased the silence told Sarah, my supervising sister below, that I was after taking one of my many breaks. She then took the handle of a brush and hammered on the kitchen ceiling to signal that progress should resume. But I figured out a plan to outmanoeuvre her. Instead of sitting down to read my book I walked back and forth producing the required noise and at the same time was able to enjoy my reading. It worked for a while until Sarah, wondering how it could take so long to do so little, crept up quietly one day, caught me unawares and discovered my ploy.

My soul rebelled against the boring, repetitive jobs around the house, but no matter how good an argument I put up as to the futility of certain tasks – and I was better at arguing than working – no argument stood a chance against my sisters' determination, so in the end they always won. Strangely enough, one of the weekly jobs from which I derived great satisfaction was cleaning the windows. This was done with newspaper and paraffin oil: the window was cleaned down first with an oil-soaked paper and then polished off with a dry one until it shone and I could see my reflection in it. The open fire accounted for much of the dirt on the windows and if the wind was in the wrong direction it might blow the smoke down the chimney, filling the kitchen. Then on the smoky panes of glass I would draw strange designs and create imagined scenes. I thought of the windows as the eyes of the house and that was probably why I felt such a sense of achievement when I cleaned them.

Every Saturday there were plenty of jobs on the agenda in preparation for Sunday. The hob was whitewashed; all the *súgán* timber chairs and the two timber tables were scrubbed white; finally, the kitchen was scrubbed out with buckets of water drawn from the spout at the end of the garden. If the voluntary workforce started to protest we were coaxed along by our shrewd older sister, Sarah, with promises of a big, juicy apple cake for tea and, like the donkey and the carrot, we kept going. She always lived up to her promises, well aware that next Saturday's tasks were only around the corner of another week. We often sang as we worked together; we laughed a lot and, like all *gearrcaigh* in the nest, we squabbled a lot as well.

The first to fly from the nest of our home was my sister Lucy, who went nursing to London. My mother was very reluctant to let her first chick head away, but my father's criterion was always: if they want to fly, let them go. Every week I wrote her long letters full of every detail of what had happened at home, and probably I wrote as much for my own satisfaction as for hers. All our lives had been so intertwined that I could not bear to think that she, who had been part of it all, should now miss out on anything. Caught up in her new life in London, she must often have smiled at the letters of a twelve-year-old with their vivid descriptions of how many chickens each hen had hatched out and the colours of all the new calves.

She came home on holidays with suitcases full of lovely clothes and, oh, the heavenly smell of rare perfume! Sometimes friends came with her, speaking in strange accents, who had never been on a farm before. I loved escorting them out around the animals and watching the reaction on their faces, especially if they stood on what they thought was firm ground but which turned out otherwise. One girl who visited on several occasions had the unusual name of Joy Love, and it was a name which suited her wonderfully because she was full of gaiety and her Scottish accent was music to the ear. She and my brother spent a lot of time talking together because they were both interested in poetry, and she sent him a book of the complete works of Robbie Burns which I came to treasure myself. It had a deep red, soft padded cover with gold lettering and gilt-edged leaves, and it slipped into its own matching holder. The pages inside were thin and flimsy with beautiful red and gold lettering at the top of every page. It gave pleasure and satisfaction before a word was ever read, and I spent many hours trying to decipher the Scottish dialect without always succeeding.

When home on holidays Lucy, who was very pretty, was never short of admirers eager to escort her. During one of these trips, in the course of which she had gone out several times with a local lad who was also home on holidays, she coolly announced that a boyfriend from London was coming to stay. Almost as an afterthought she added that she was thinking of getting engaged to him. This, as far as my mother was concerned, was completely out of line. In her reckoning, if you were that serious about one man you cleared the field of all other contenders. But her oldest daughter had other ideas, so a long argument commenced.

"We know nothing about this fellow," said my mother, with the implication in her voice that, since we did not, there might be something wrong with him.

"Well, what do you want to know?" came the reply.

"What does he do? What are his family like? What religion is he?"

When my mother stopped to draw breath Lucy chimed in, "He's a medical student in the hospital where I work; he has one brother and his parents are very nice; and he doesn't believe in anything."

"Holy mother of divine God!" my father exclaimed as he grabbed his cap and made for the kitchen door to go out to his animals, which he found a lot easier to understand than his daughters.

My mother was determined to get to the root of the matter. "How do you mean he doesn't believe in anything? Where does he think he came from?" she demanded.

My sister was too smart to get caught in a theological debate with my mother, so she soothed her down by asking her to reserve judgement until the subject of their argument appeared on the scene. An uneasy truce was agreed, which Lucy did nothing to cement when she went dancing again with her local friend that night.

A few days later our man from London arrived and revealed himself to be a very precise, English gentleman of few words, who had probably never seen a cow in his life before. I was fascinated by him. Anybody who did not believe in God was a great novelty and it was rather disappointing to find that he looked ordinary enough, except for his well-cut country tweeds, which might have been very suitable for an English hunt but not for Irish country roads. After a few days he began to thaw out and we discovered a very charming young man beneath his crisp, correct exterior.

When he returned to London he sent my mother a huge box of flowers. They were the first she ever got that she had not grown herself, as my father had never been inclined to say it with flowers. Their arrival at the local bus-stop created a bit of excitement. There was a pub at the bus-stop where the kindly publican, Jim, looked after all sorts of miscellaneous objects, from parts for ploughs to bundles of blankets, but a box of fresh flowers added a new dimension to his responsibilities for, while most things could be left there indefinitely without creating a problem, these had to be shifted before they started to wilt. Another difficulty was that most merchandise arriving by bus had been sent for and the person who had ordered it would come and collect it. The arrival of the flowers, however, had no precedent and was totally unexpected. But we, like everyone in rural Ireland, possessed a local communication system which soon solved the problem. Jim sent a message to Pat in the Post Office to tell Martin the postman to call to us the following morning to let us know that the flowers were lying in state on the pub counter. It probably took the flowers longer to get to our home from the bus-stop than it took them to come from London, but we got them in the end.

My father collected them on his way from the creamery the following day and the huge oblong box stretched like a cardboard coffin across the three churns of milk. On his arrival home the box was borne aloft into the parlour, where it was laid out on the big oak table. The entire household, including visiting cousins and helpers, gathered to witness the opening ceremony. My mother untied the ribbons with the air of reverence she normally reserved for her rosary beads. She gently folded back the layers and layers of soft, white tissue-paper and there they were, rows and rows of the most gorgeous gladioli. My sister Phil spoke all our thoughts when she breathed, "That guy certainly knows how to impress!"

For days afterwards we had gladioli standing upright in every vase and jug, filling the parlour and kitchen. In later years whenever I saw gladioli I remembered the man my sister might have married.

The Royal Wee

THE MIRACLE OF modern plumbing is difficult to appreciate for those who have never known its predecessors, but for those of us who grew up with the chamber-pot and po for companions the flush toilet came as a modern marvel. Indeed, if there had been an award for the invention that best filled a gap in the market it should surely have gone to the man or woman who invented the flush toilet.

One came into our house shortly after the advent of electricity when my father harnessed a free-flowing spring that poured down the hill behind the house and put it to a more practical use. Old Tom, when he viewed it in action, declared, "Be the hokey but that's a mighty yoke when you can flush everything down a hole. That could give a man the idea that he is no longer responsible for his actions."

When Jim in the local pub installed an outdoor model that operated by pulling a chain it created great excitement. One old man sat on it for the first time and pulled the dangling chain, quite unprepared for the consequences; in his ensuing panic he ran into the pub, his trousers at half mast, shouting that the whole place was going to be flooded.

Its ancestor, the humble po, led a sheltered existence in obscure corners and shadowy places. It was seldom mentioned in polite society, yet it was the one household item that straddled all social barriers and was essential in every dwelling, from the humble cottage to the royal palace. But even within the po democracy there were different social layers. At the bottom of the ladder came the humble white enamel model with a navy blue or red rim and matching handle. This was the poor man's po. They could be stacked on top of each other and could withstand rough treatment, though when this happened and the enamel got chipped care had to be taken lest adjoining enamel become embedded in vital points of the anatomy, causing a certain amount of discomfort. Next on the social ladder came the plain white ware model, but in recognition of its middle-class status its title changed from plain "po" to rather more euphonious "chamber-pot". The chamber-pot was a fine, solid, serviceable job. It had no tendency to chip and only if you dropped it on the hard stone floor did it crack. My grandmother opted for one of these, but because the ordinary po position was beneath her dignity she ensconced it in a mahogany chair called a commode, which had a false bottom into which the chamber-pot withdrew.

The chamber-pot had as working companions a large ware jug and a basin. Because there was no water on tap this jug was filled from the rain-water barrel daily and the water was then poured into the large bowl for washing when necessary. You washed in cold water unless you had a retinue of servants to draw hot water for you. After washing, the water was poured into a white enamel bucket and later taken out and emptied.

All this action took place at the dressing-table, which might have a circular hole on top into which the basin fitted or, more commonly, it might have a marble top and a colourfully tiled back. Underneath some dressing-tables was a closed-off section with a little door, inside which the chamber-pot lived in seclusion. Beside the jug and bowl on top there were usually a matching soap dish and shaving mug, and sometimes a bone container for the male's studs.

At the top of the market a high-class chamber-pot blossomed into flowers, usually pink roses or blue forget-me-nots. Its bedroom companions sported the same colours and were quite decorative; some were colour co-ordinated with paintwork as well. Some boasted embossed flowers and were works of art in the variety and intricacy of their design and colour. In some houses a special chamber-pot, ornate and not intended for ordinary bottoms, was reserved for visitors.

Emptying the po was an exercise that had to be carried out daily and this delicate operation was performed by the senior females of the household after they had first established that no unexpected visitors were within the precincts. My grandmother, if she had misjudged the situation and found herself approached by someone who was where he should not have been, whipped her long black apron into action, covering all before her. The fact that at seventy-five this gave her a decidedly pregnant look did not disturb her in the least.

When she had visitors and wanted to know if they needed to avail of her chamber-pot facilities she asked, "Would you like to sit down?" and "Would you like to tidy yourself?" On first hearing this politely worded invitation I was somewhat confused, as I observed that the lady to whom my grandmother had addressed her questions was already sitting down and looked quite tidy. However, I knew my grandmother well enough not to question the appropriateness of her terminology and after a while I managed to figure out her meaning.

One neighbour had occasion to use her chamber-pot to dampen unwelcome male ardour. A drunken visitor refused to stop knocking on her front door in the small hours of the morning. After repeated attempts to persuade him to depart she finally, in a fit of temper, opened a window above the front door and baptised his head with a mixed blessing, which proved most effective in speeding him on his way. Another old neighbour, when the handle fell off his ware chamber-pot, used it as a money box and still kept it under the bed.

The same old man used a new chamber-pot he had in reserve to solve the problem of some unwelcome visitors. They had invited themselves to stay with him and he was at his wits' end as to how he could shift them when he got a brainwave. He brought out the new chamber-pot, but pretended that it was the one from under his bed. Then he placed it on the kitchen table and proceeded to wash the ware in it. His visitors made a hasty exit.

The po might have many titles: those with a musical bent called it "the piano", those with literary notions "the Edgar Allan" and those with medical inclinations "the vessel". We children called it "the jerry-pot" and those with no respect at all called it "the piss-pot". But the title that appealed most to me was that given to it by my dear old friend Molly who termed it "the goesees-under".

The once-humble chamber-pot has since climbed into the exalted realms of the world of antiques, which it graces as a collectors' item. At an auction recently a Wedgewood model fetched a handsome price and I smiled, thinking of its late owner, an eccentric old gentleman who had refused to transport his fragile anatomy to the modern wonder of the flush toilet, maintaining that the po position kept things properly in motion. Now his precious po was destined to become an expensive flower-pot, and I had no doubt he would have considered it a fitting end for so serviceable an item.

Home Drama

A TRIP TO Cork City assumed for me as a child the momentous importance of a journey to a foreign country, and it was on one of these rare and wonderful excursions that I discovered books. A collection of hardback classics which I found on the shelves of Woolworths provided me with a passport to another world. I drew my books home from the city one by one and, if funds were unusually plentiful, I might sometimes stretch my haul to two. I cried at the hungry plight of poor Oliver Twist and rejoiced at his final escape into a better life. I moved enthusiastically on through other books by Dickens, relishing his characters, but all of these paled into insignificance when the territory of my reading shifted northwards; I came across the brooding Brontës and was drawn into the absorbing tension between the correct behaviour of their time and the powerful undercurrents of dark, wild passion which was embodied in their writing. I read and re-read their books until I felt I had a personal relationship with the entire family and believed that I could easily find my way around their isolated house and across the lonely moors. The only respect in which the world of the Brontës disappointed me was in its cold, detached father who failed to match up, I felt, to our colourful and dramatic man, who sometimes stretched our patience to the limit but around whom there was never a dull moment.

These popular classics had cream-coloured covers, were printed on soft cream paper and were well bound so that they did not fall apart. Their smell when new was of another world, a world of the imagination, and I loved it so much I would run my nose up and down the pages to inhale their essence. I found that just as some gardens offered welcomes with their fragrances and some houses had their special atmospheres, the feel and smell of a new book was an indication of the life within. The books in Woolworths cost three shillings each, an amount which was hard to come by, and my appetite for reading seemed always to outstrip my supply of coins, so I was constantly in search of opportunities to earn some pay for special jobs at home.

We children bargained with my father for so much per drill for thinning turnips and picking potatoes, and sometimes we had to threaten strike action to extract our earnings. If a calf, a bonham or a lamb was sickly – an *íochtar* – we became foster-parents and staked our claim for a share of the price when they were sold. Another source of revenue was "stands", as we called them: visiting friends and relations often put their hands in their pockets and withdrew a brown or silver coin. Brown was the usual story but occasionally we might get silver and then we struck oil, for a shilling had a lot of spending in it and a half-crown was riches indeed. A friend of my father's, who was having a pint with him one fair day, gave me a half-crown and I could hardly believe my eyes. I never forgot his kindness and the way he smiled and said "enjoy spending it", and I did indeed because it became the down payment on my much-prized copy of *Little Women*. Years later I travelled many miles to be at the funeral of the man who gave me the key to the world of Louisa May Alcott.

We did not own a car, and neither did any of our

neighbours, but there was a hackney-man in town who went to Cork weekly or sometimes even twice weekly if he had a load. There was also a bus, and this set out early each morning, returning late at night, but its route wound through a wide swathe of surrounding countryside, so the hackney-car was first choice for comfort and convenience. Jim the hackney-man was also the publican, so we waited on high bar stools for him to drive us to Cork, sipping fizzy brown lemonade and watching the old men drinking their frothy black pints as we waited. Like most pubs it did not restrict itself to selling drinks, and this was also the place to buy needles, hairpins and elastic. Jim was very much a part of our lives, as well as of our neighbours'; unfailingly patient and pleasant, he was a storyteller who could shorten any journey. He was involved in most of the important events in the lives of the people of the neighbourhood because he drove us to and from weddings, funerals, christenings and other family occasions. During his years as hackney-driver he had witnessed the life stories of many families, but he treated every family as his own and was never known to divulge a confidence. Being so aware of the goings-on in families and being so understanding with it, he was often called upon to sort out family tangles. Once when Lucy, home on holidays, was complaining about her earnings as a newly qualified nurse he asked her how much she was being paid; she told him and he just said quietly, "Many a man is keeping a wife and children on that". She was glad later that he had put matters in perspective for her.

With every trip in the hackney-car to Cork my collection of books grew and soon I felt the need for a special corner for them. At the top of the house was an old attic which we called the black loft because it was poorly lit by one small dormer window and a tiny deep one in the gable-end overlooking the grove. When we were small we sometimes squeezed through this window, which led onto the roof of the old stone turf-house and from there down into the grove, but later we outgrew its miniature proportions. The dormer window was the better of the two because it had a view out over the fields: from here I could see the old stone school – from a safe distance – and the little bridge over the river that crept along between high banks, forming a natural boundary between neighbouring farms.

The black loft was my retreat corner and I created a world of my own there amongst the relics of the past: the family cradle and the brass cot, both of which I, as the youngest in the family, had been the last to occupy; the butter churns and the horse tackling – too far gone for use but awaiting repair some wet day unless it might find its way eventually to the harness-maker. The plaster on the walls was crumbling and rafters bared themselves under the roof; the floorboards sagged, revealing the ceiling of the room below and making it essential to step gently to avoid a hasty and unpremeditated exit to the lower regions.

Three steps led down to the black loft from my parents' bedroom, which was in a newer part of the house which had been built above the level of the old house. Just inside the door of the loft a sagging rafter could catch unwary visitors and easily render them unconscious. At the far end stairs led down into a room below the parlour, which was used as a spare room and had bay windows opening into the garden. Thus I had more than one exit when seeking to escape from undesirable chores, even though the stairs at the far end were officially closed due to their dangerous condition. I loved the thrill of using it as an emergency exit; swinging past the gaps I relished the excitement of knowing that if I fell into one of the black holes beneath me I might never be seen again.

HOME DRAMA

Mice had made the place their own, so when I was about to enter I always gave them prior notice by flinging one of my father's boots in before me, and they duly scattered in all directions and out of respect for my presence never invaded my privacy. They were less considerate, however, in their habit of leaving evidence of their visitations. Also, they had an unfortunate appetite for our home-made glue, a paste of flour and water which they seemed to regard not at all as an adhesive but as a heaven-sent source of sustenance. Had it not been for impenetrable iron trunks, many a scrapbook and home-made picture would have been destroyed by them.

Scrapbooks provided the perfect medium for paying private homage to the glamorous film stars of the time, and one of my hobbies was collecting movie magazines and compiling scrapbooks about my favourite stars. Elizabeth Taylor, Ava Gardner and Rita Hayworth shone as foremost beauties while Stewart Grainger, Montgomery Clift and Clark Gable were the dashing male heroes. Sometimes on summer evenings after the cows had been milked we walked to the cinema in town to see some of the stars in action. My mother did not entirely approve of all these bare-breasted beauties, nor their frequent changing of husbands, but when I showed an interest in the British royal family she was much more positive, feeling that even if they were rather far removed from us, at least their morals were apparently above reproach.

I was denied the luxury of a bedroom of my own because demand exceeded availability, so I shared with sisters and with many visiting cousins during the holidays, and this often led to chatting which continued far into the night until my father thumped on the timber partition and eventually silenced us. But nobody else bothered with the black loft and so it became my private domain. In the summer it was very hot and in the winter it was freezing, and because the window did not shut properly the weather outside sometimes found its way in. High winds sprayed raindrops in and blizzards whirled snowflakes through to fall like thistledown on the bare, dusty floor. The conditions, however, did not deter me, and it was here on a woodworm-eaten and wobbly table with one short leg that I wrote my first story.

My sisters and I underwent a phase of impromptu home drama. To begin with we used the kitchen as our stage, the room off it serving as our dressing-room, but as we progressed we found these arangements too amateurish and so we moved to an empty loft over the stalls. This loft was normally used for storing straw but was empty between seasons. We put it to good use. Old curtains that belonged to the parlour were rigged up and props collected from all over the farm.

We lacked a script so we made it up as we went along, which often resulted in the cast becoming involved in long, heated arguments on stage because their dialogue was failing to coordinate. Then an intermission was called and the whole thing was gone through before we started in again. We were an ad lib, think-as-you-go-along theatre group, and as the audience for one show could be on stage for the following one we tended to restrain our criticisms. Sometimes we might purport to present a play that we had heard on the radio, but if the playwright had happened along he might not have recognized it as his work.

We whiled away many a wet day up in that loft until my mother decided to turn it into a hen-house, to which we strongly objected, but our needs were of no importance in comparison to the needs of the hens, so for the summer we moved out of doors and performed under the trees in the grove behind the house. The only constant supporter we had was our old friend Bill, who came up with helpful prompts when any actress ran out of lines. He was a most accommodating audience. My father refused to allow us to move our theatre group into the black loft, which was my suggestion, as he was afraid that in the excitement of high drama we might forget the sagging floorboards and one of us put our foot in the wrong place and come down through the parlour ceiling. So we remained a mobile theatre group and whichever stall, stable or pig-house was available, we moved in, though sometimes we had to put a lot of work into eradicating the aroma of the previous residents.

I made gallant efforts to provide plays for our performances but they were taken apart on stage and rewritten to suit individual performers. The cast was entirely female as my brother had set up his own boxing club which had declared an empty corner of the barn their boxing ring. Sometimes when there was no play on we became the ringside audience, shouting on whichever of the champions we favoured.

When I first saw boxing gloves I was intrigued by the size of them and sometimes when my brother needed a sparring partner I donned the gloves and learned to dance around and duck and weave. He usually used a punch-bag which hung off the rafters of the barn for practice but he assured me that I was slightly better. We developed an interest in boxing championships then and gathered around the radio to follow the fortunes of Joe Louis and Bruce Woodcock and other champions of the ring, especially the Irish ones. The night that Rinty Monaghan became world champion and sang "When Irish Eyes Are Smiling" we all danced around the kitchen with glee, and we followed with the greatest of interest the career of our own local hero, Irish middle-weight champion Pat O'Connor.

The black loft remained the corner where I spent

time on my own. In the spring when the swallows came they refurbished their old nests under the roof beside the window and I watched them swishing in and out. In the evenings during the summer months I might sit inside the little window to watch the shadows slanting across the fields and listen to the corncrake playing the same tune non-stop like a record with the needle stuck. The monotonous regularity of his voice merged into the chorus of night voices so completely that sometimes I was quite unaware that he had stopped.

In our family we all felt the need for our own places to which we could retreat from time to time and often as I looked out from my perch at the top of the house in the quiet of the evening I would see my father walking down the fields to his own particular spot by the river. I liked to watch him saunter along with his hands in his pockets, his cap pushed to the back of his head and the dogs with him chasing rabbits, real and imaginary, through the bushes. That was his relaxation time when he went, the cares of the day behind him, down to his favourite place to watch the fish jump and to listen to the sounds of the countryside.

A Marriage
Of Convenience

MIKE AND MAUD had a small farm on the hill across the river from our house. They were too far afield to be on my visiting list as a child but as I grew older the distance became shorter. Mike had been well into his fifties before he had decided that a wife might add to the flavour of his life, but because a do-it-yourself effort had never appealed to him he had simply let it be known in the right places that he was available and hoped that somebody suitable would feel that he was just what she wanted. He was quite realistic about his requirements and about what he had to offer. As he described it later, he was not in the market for "a flighty young one who would burn me out in no time at all". What he wanted was companionship with a mild bit of excitement thrown in, and he was quite emphatic about the small measure of the excitement because he needed reserves for his greyhounds, who were the great love of his life. Indeed, the one essential qualification he did insist on was that his future wife should love his dogs as himself. In due course his greyhound contacts came up with the answer; being doggy people themselves they knew exactly what Mike was looking for, and thus Maud came into his life.

They had been married for over twenty years when I first started visiting them. Mike loved to tell the story of how Maud had come to be his wife. According to him

Maud had a sister and it was she he had met first; they had decided to get married but she had had a cold on the morning of the wedding and so Maud had come instead. Maud for her part neither contradicted nor confirmed his story, only shaking her head and saying, "We must listen to the wind that falls the houses", and maybe that was the secret of their happy marriage. Mike felt free to live like a bachelor while Maud ran the farm. He had never had any great interest in work, whereas she had shared the running of a small, mountainy farm with a sister and two brothers and she had the desire and ability to carry far more responsibility. "She likes to get her head," Mike constantly remarked approvingly; being of a leisurely disposition himself, he had great admiration for industrious people, despite having no wish to imitate them. He was tolerant and Maud was pleasant and good-natured and, as Mike said, "her heart was in the right place".

Mike had received little formal education but he had a great interest in the wonders of nature and the movements of the planets. When one of our neighbour's sons qualified as a teacher he gave night classes in the local school for people such as Mike, who had missed out on schooling and were keen to broaden their fields of knowledge. An interested and interesting collection of students, young Dan the teacher must have found them quite a contrast to his day pupils. One night he was endeavouring to explain to them, with the help of a globe, about the world turning on its axis and the regularity with which this took place, but it was too much for Mike who slapped the bench with his hand.

"Will you for God's sake, Dan, talk a bit of sense. I'm over there on that farm with seventy-five years," he exclaimed, pointing out of the school window in the direction of his own place, "and the bloody ground never stirred an inch."

A MARRIAGE OF CONVENIENCE

When electricity came Mike was fascinated by all the gadgets that came with it, and his was the first electric blanket in our part of the country. He also purchased an electric clock and was delighted with the fact that it kept perfect time. For years he had been at the mercy of a temperamental alarm clock that, a little like himself, decided to take a rest every so often. The alarm clock had been used in both the kitchen and bedroom but now it was placed on permanent bedroom duty while the new electric clock took over in the kitchen. One wet day Mike decided to investigate the reason why the alarm clock kept such bad time. Maud had gone into town and he had the place to himself; he pulled the kitchen table up close to the fire, sat himself down in comfort and proceeded to dismantle the clock. Every little screw and wheel was taken apart and laid out on a newspaper on the table, and Mike passed an enjoyable few hours studying the intricacies of his timepiece. He had taken careful note of every piece in the process of dismantling, yet when he had put it all back together again he found that he was left with one spare part.

"Do you know something," he said to Maud, "it's no wonder that clock kept bad time: the fool that made it put in an extra wheel." The clock, of course, never ticked again.

Mike and Maud had no children because, as he put it, time was against them, a fact for which he was eternally grateful. He suffered from no unfulfilled paternal longings, unlike his neighbour and friend Pat O'Shea, who lamented his lack of a son and heir in verse:

> Fine green fields
> And no one for them;
> She fooled poor Pat O'Shea:
> She said she was
> Twenty years and four
> But she was forty years

And far more.
She fooled poor Pat O'Shea:
My fine green fields
And no one for them.

Mike gave Pat very little sympathy and he always said that what Maud did with the land when he died was entirely up to her. And when he did die, his last words to Maud were to mind his greyhounds.

As with everything he did, Mike took death in his stride. One morning he was not feeling well so he stayed in bed, and at lunch-time he just closed his eyes and died. Maud was not one to panic, so in due course she sent for Mrs Casey to lay him out. As she was passing our house Mrs Casey called for my mother and when they arrived at Mike's my mother talked to Maud while Mrs Casey went into the bedroom. After a few more neighbours had arrived Mrs Casey beckoned my mother into the bedroom.

"There is something wrong here," she announced. "He is not cooling down."

"What on earth do you mean?" my mother asked in surprise.

"Mike is dead long enough to be getting cold, but he's not. I've laid out many a dead man and I know how dead men act and Mike isn't acting like a dead man."

"But he must be dead," my mother insisted, not knowing quite how to handle this development. "He looks dead anyway."

"Well, he doesn't feel dead," Mrs Casey said, putting her hand on Mike. As they pondered their dilemma Maud entered the room and saw the two of them looking at Mike.

"What's wrong?" she asked. "Why are ye not laying him out?"

"The way it is, Maud," Mrs Casey explained, "Mike is hot and he should be cold."

A MARRIAGE OF CONVENIENCE

"Oh," Maud said, looking puzzled and going towards the bed. She examined Mike and the bed and then her face cleared and she smiled. "Well, the old devil," she exclaimed, "he had the electric blanket plugged in – he loved the comfort of it." And going to the foot of the bed she unplugged Mike and Mrs Casey was able to get on with her job.

Maud died a few years after Mike and now their little house is in ruins. They had gone into marriage with no great expectations on either side, yet their home had always been full of contentment and good humour.

"Come Home Dacent"

NOTHING COULD COMPETE for excitement with the carnival, which came to town every year in June. We lined the street waiting eagerly for the fancy-dress parade, squealing with excitement when it came into view and straining our eyes to identify the mysterious locals dressed up in their costume disguises. The carnival queen, with her glittering tiara and her ladies-in-waiting dressed in frothy, full-length gowns, was the ultimate in glamour and the envy of all the little girls dressed, as we were, in our sun-bleached hand-me-downs. The parade over, we went to the "merries", where we swung high in the swinging boats and chased each other around the big spinner, inside which dolls and sets of ware competed with each other to tempt mothers and fathers.

My father did not go to the carnival but sat at home and smoked his pipe by the kitchen fire, grateful for the rare pleasure of having the house to himself. On such occasions he never lit the lamp but sat in the gathering dusk, the only light being the yellow flicker of the turf fire and the red glow of his pipe. When we returned home at about midnight we burst into his silent domain, regaling him with stories of money lost and won on pongo, of rides on the merries, of the excitement of our day, and patiently he listened to us before seizing an opportunity to escape upstairs to bed.

"COME HOME DACENT"

We left the carnival field as night was falling, but before we headed for home we gathered around the door of the old ballroom which stood over a garage in a field. The field was hilly and the garage seemed to burrow into the hill at the rear while the dance-hall rode on its back, its doors opening onto the street. We watched open-mouthed while older sisters and neighbouring girls with curled hair went in, all dressed in swirling skirts. Curls were the fashion and nobody would admit to straight hair except the old ladies who caught their hair into a knot or "cuck" at the base of the poll. How we envied those glamorous girls, and when the door opened and we caught a glimpse into the hall itself it was a sight from another world. Glittering balls hung from the ceiling, the floor shone with a maple sheen, and bursts of familiar tunes escaped with each swing of the door. We were well versed in the music of the day and the band was playing all our tunes; Guy Mitchell provided the foot-tapping numbers, while Frankie Lane and Nat King Cole slowed the tempo.

Finally we were dragged away by my mother or a neighbour, or else my sister Sarah came to the door of the dance-hall to dispatch us all off home. If we had any pennies left we called into a little shop that stayed open late for the carnival and pooled our resources to buy a bar of chocolate for the road home. A full bar of chocolate was an unheard-of luxury, so one bar was broken up into squares and shared around, and sometimes squares had to be further divided so that everyone could have a bit. The miracle of the loaves and fishes was no miracle to us.

We walked up the old road, as the road home was called, and the strains of the music became fainter, soon to be replaced by the call of the corncrake and the occasional crow of the cock pheasant. The moon shone down, lighting up the road ahead and throwing the hedges into shadow; we enjoyed imagining that all sorts of spooks lurked in these shadows, and this often triggered off an unplanned race along the road. When we ran out of breath we staggered to a halt and sat on a mossy ditch to recover; here we told each other stories or, if the girls outnumbered the boys, we planned what we would wear at our first dance when we were old enough. Starting off again we lapsed into silence for a few minutes and could hear the cows snorting and munching grass inside the ditches. We leaned against an iron gate and some of us climbed up to sit on top and watch the cows in the moonlight. We seldom saw the countryside this late at night and it had an eerie stillness under the moon, with the farmhouses huddled on the hills and trees crouched on the horizon like dark, shadowy figures.

* * * *

And then the years had passed, the carnival was in town again and I was sixteen, quivering in anticipation of my first dance, waiting to take my first step into a new and exciting world. I was just finishing my Inter Cert exams and the last subjects received scant attention as the other girls and I planned our big night. We tried on each other's dresses, skirts and blouses, each seeking the magic combination which would show her off to her best advantage.

To me the unattainable dream was a low-cut dress with sufficient cleavage inside it to keep it afloat. But, at a time when fashion demanded round-bosomed, curvaceous female bodies, I suffered the pangs of adolescence, yearning to be other than I was, with my long legs and my body so thin that my grandmother had told me I was like the stroke of 1 on a sheet of paper.

One of my friends, on hearing of my fervent aspiration to display a plunging neckline, brought me a bright red, scanty dress which belonged to an aunt of hers who was home on holidays from London. It was the last word in sophistication: I was about to become a scarlet woman, the fulfilment of all my dreams. But when I waltzed into the kitchen with this flimsy model high above my knees and cut so low that it displayed what I had not got, my mother nearly had heart failure. My sister Sarah pronounced a sarcastic verdict of "dressed-up tart", and my father, as he passed through the kitchen, scratched his head and muttered something about a "hoor's top". And it was there in the kitchen that my red dress was whipped off me, wrapped up in a brown paper bag and thrust back into my schoolbag beneath my books. I was sent off to school on the last day of my exams with my only hope of becoming a scarlet woman buried beneath Virgil and Shakespeare. I had always been impressed by the tragedy of Lady MacBeth, but that day her tragedy seemed pale by comparison with mine.

After trying on black taffeta shirts with white frilly blouses and miscellaneous dresses, all of us first-timers got ourselves sorted out. Ownership posed no problem: we pooled our resources and a democratic vote decided who looked best in what. It was unanimously decided that a white dress with a shower of pale pink roses looked best on me, and once the decision had been reached I resolved that if I could not be red and devastating then I would be pale and interesting. In fact, I was going to be the most pale and interesting girl who ever went to a dance, and so intent was I on creating this image that I refused to go out in the sun, hoping that my tan would fade and my freckles disappear. I had read in Sarah's copy of *Woman's Weekly* that a face-pack of flake meal whitened the skin and removed blemishes.

143

The beauty expert who had written this sterling piece of advice had no doubt assumed that only normal people read her column, people who would be intelligent enough to carry out the operation just once a week. But she had not reckoned on an enthusiastic sixteen-year-old determined to become ashen-faced within a week.

I pursued my beautification programme under a tree, in the suitable seclusion of a grove behind the house. Here I wedged between the two lowest branches of a tree a jagged piece of broken mirror advertising Irish Whiskey and examined my appearance. I had to angle my face sideways in order to get a good view of it in between the R in Irish and the W in Whiskey below. As I tilted my head lumps of the caked flake meal that I had applied to my face fell to the ground and the hens from the nearby hen-house gratefully gobbled it up. My dedicated beauty therapy came to an abrupt end, however, when my mother decided to investigate the reason why her large jar of flake meal for the morning porridge had been reduced to such a low ebb. It seemed I was destined not to be pale and interesting either.

Everyone else was going into curls for the big night but my hair was too long so I had to opt for plaits. Until I had reached fourteen my hair had been pure blonde but when I needed it to look its best it decided to go a strange-looking brown. To remedy this for my dancing debut and to recover my former flaxen glory, I purchased a bottle of peroxide in the local chemist's shop but, before I could achieve my objective, my mother thwarted me again. I was striving desperately to make myself beautiful but my mother was equally determined to keep me the way I was. Quietly and firmly she outmanoeuvered me at all points and, despite my tantrums and tears, she never lost her cool. In the end the only course open to me was to plait my long hair and coil it around my head; at least that way there would not be too much of it on view.

Before venturing onto the dance-floor it was obviously necessary to learn to dance, and this responsibility my sisters undertook with determination and great insensitivity. Propelled around the kitchen, I was forced to reverse into complicated semi-circles that made me feel that my legs and head had suffered a breakdown of communications. No suitable records were available to play on the gramophone because my father's repertoire favoured John McCormack and Delia Murphy. "The Old House" and "If I Was A Blackbird" were not exactly ideal for the quick-steps and sambas that I was supposed to master. This left the radio as the sole source of our ballroom dancing music. Victor Sylvester on the BBC had a whole hour of ballroom dancing, but an hour was not enough so, when any suitable music came on, the sister on kitchen duty ran to the front door and blew the whistle that was normally used to summon men in from the fields for meals, thus sometimes creating a false alarm. I was expected to come running, even if the whistle sounded at the most inopportune moments, and on many occasions I left a half-fed calf bellowing in protest as I raced for the kitchen, casting wellingtons ahead of me so as to have my feet free for action. Often I would not make it in time: the dance music had died and my flight had been in vain. If my father happened to witness any of these performances, and especially if he had answered a false alarm, he would take off his cap, scratch his head, cast his eyes to heaven and exclaim: "Lord, pity the man who has five daughters!"

The morning of the big event dawned at last. Those who wanted to curl straight hair had had to commence operations the previous night, rolling their hair up in little tin curling pins called dinkies for the tight look or donning huge spiky rollers to achieve a softer effect. These devices were not, of course, conducive to sound sleep and those who used them paid a price for their curly looks; as my father remarked, it was like going to bed with their heads in barbed wire. Some brave individuals went to Mass without taking out their rollers but wrapped scarves around their swollen, lumpy heads. Older people disapproved of this and peers, especially those of the opposite sex, often passed caustic remarks, leading the unfortunate girls to find out how difficult it was to treat a comment with contempt when your head was twice its normal size.

After the last Mass that Sunday the troops gathered when pals came together as much for the shared anticipation as for the final dress-rehearsal. But first body reclamation began: under-arm fuzz was mowed down with a safety razor stolen from my brother while he was out; we passed it around and it soon lost its edge but one resourceful young lady had a packet of blades which allowed us to continue the hair eradication programme. Legs were inspected, some were declared ripe for harvesting, and once we got started nothing was safe. Eyebrows were trimmed to near-extinction and some hairstyles deemed to be not quite right came under attack from scissors, often with disastrous results.

Next we turned to underwear. We had recently discovered the wonderful world of the bra: some because they were too richly endowed, others because they sought to give themselves what God had not, by recourse to "falsies" or by stuffing their bras with hankies. Our inexperienced manouevres with our bras provoked high entertainment and we spent more time laughing than fitting them on. Stockings were even more novel, for up to now we had always gone bare-legged about the farm, and when I saw my first suspender-belt it reminded me immediately of a pony's tackling.

The long-legged knickers my mother favoured were cast aside for flimsy silk panties, very brief, with lace edging around the ends. Not quite trusting the delicate elastic, I got a good firm type from my mother's work box and with a safety-pin re-threaded the band; I was determined to avoid the experience of an older friend who one night had suddenly felt that what should have been around her hips were now down around her ankles. The dance-floor had been crowded and nobody had noticed, so she had smartly stepped out of them and whipped them up, slipping them unobtrusively into the jacket pocket of her dancing partner, who later had quite a surprise when he reached for his cigarettes.

Our activities were brought to an abrupt end when my father banged on the kitchen ceiling with the handle of a brush and demanded to know if there was anyone to bring in the cows for milking, to feed the hens and the calves, or had we all taken leave of our senses and did we want him to sell out the whole place and buy a dance-hall. A mad scramble ensued and we all scattered in different directions to get the various jobs done while neighbouring pals ran home across the ditches to do likewise. The cows were gallopped home across the fields; buckets of milk were slapped under calves' heads, and hens and chickens were rounded up to be fed. The jobs completed in record time, we gathered in the kitchen for supper, which had been hastily prepared by the sister on duty there. Supper finished and ware washed, we resumed the real business of the evening: getting ready for the dance. Dress-rehearsal over, the live show was about to begin.

In various corners of the house we scrubbed ourselves down over enamel dishes and buckets. Then we gathered in the upstairs front bedroom where the beds were buried deep beneath our dresses, skirts, blouses and frilly underskirts. First bras and suspender-belts were fastened, and those who wanted to look thinner than they were squeezed themselves into corsets with much gasping and breathing in. Next came the delicate operation of easing fine nylons over our legs, while avoiding the tragedy of a ladder, before hitching them to suspenders. Then we drew on our panties, about which old Tom aptly remarked that they did not provide much shelter.

The next garment under the dress was a slip. An interlock one served the purpose and a silk one was the last word in elegance, but without a slip one was considered not quite respectable. It was the style of the times that every dress should billow forth, and so over the slip went an underskirt of stiff, white net to provide the necessary support. Then came the dress, about which so much agonizing had gone on for days, and the sandals, which were usually white. All that remained to be attended to was the face, and the secret here was to put on enough make-up to erase the scrubbed and shiny look but little enough to escape my mother's inspection. One stick of pancake make-up, one box of face-powder and one tube of lipstick covered all shapes and shades of faces. An imaginative friend discovered that the red cover of her father's creamery book, in which butter and milk sales were recorded, could be dampened and used as rouge, but my mother promptly made her wash it off. My dreams were of the full scarlet mouth of Ava Gardner and the smouldering, black-lined eyes of Joan Crawford, but my mother made sure that they remained just dreams. Cussons talcum powder, in a little orange-and-white box, was as near as we came to perfume, so we shook it in all corners.

Finally, leaving the bedroom in chaos, we trooped downstairs into the kitchen where my parents and a few of the neighbours, including Tom, waited to put us through a passing-out parade. Many good-humoured comments were passed and we girls gave as good as we got. But old Tom remained silent, puffing his pipe in a cloud of smoke until we were going out the door. Then he delivered a parting shot: "Come home dacent," was all he said.

We walked the three miles into town, joining up with other young people along the way, singing and practising our steps as we went. At that stage I had an attack of first-night nerves. What if my legs refused to keep time to the music? What if nobody asked me to dance? What if my panties fell down? The possibilities of disaster seemed endless and I almost envied the children buying chocolate for the road home, but not quite, because just then we came within range of the sound of music and my heart started to beat with a fierce new excitement.

Sarah had appointed herself cashier, so she went to buy the tickets and the rest of us queued up behind her like ducks going to a pond. As I waited in line I thought of all the instructions that had been hammered into me by my sisters and their friends: Don't get stuck with one fellow for the night; avoid drunks by keeping a weather eye out for them and getting lost in the crowd when you saw one coming; dance with everyone but if somebody turned up who was beyond endurance say you had the dance promised to someone else. I was beginning to feel that the Inter Cert had been a walkover compared with this test of diplomatic skills.

Sarah, having procured the tickets, propelled us forward and, once inside the door, we were soon enfolded in a warm world full of swirling couples, coloured lights, pulsating music and the smell of paraffin oil and sawdust. We made our way to the cloakroom, where we hung up our coats. Here older girls preened themselves in front of cracked mirrors and straightened the seams in their stockings. Comments like "God, he nearly crippled me" and "Hope he'll ask me to dance again" floated through the powdered air and a feeling of gaiety and sisterhood prevailed. We first-timers were welcomed and cautioned about "the octopus", "the prancing jennet" and the handsome "scalp collector"; the research team was voluntary, caring and anxious that we young ones should enjoy ourselves and avoid the tried and tested male hazards.

Outside the cloakroom was a sea of girls and I wondered where the men were hiding, until I made my way out to the front, and there across the hall were rows of men, a bewildering array of them. Before I could decide who I hoped would ask me to dance a school-friend came over as the band started up, saying, "Come on and I'll see if your dancing is better than your algebra". The dance-hall floor was a great improvement on the stone floor of the kitchen, and with the live music and a partner who obviously knew what to do with his legs my dancing problem faded fast as the music went in through my ears and out through my toes. I was sorry when that first dance was over because this lad who but a few weeks previously had been just a classroom companion was now a smiling, entertaining young man. The atmosphere of soft lights and soothing music put our friendship on a new and altogether more interesting footing, and I decided that after the holidays school would never be as boring again.

After a few dances I realized that most of our school was there and also many of the neighbours, so I relaxed and felt that if this was what dancing was all about it was great fun. Then a blond, very handsome man in his twenties asked me to dance. This guy was a different model from the others and when the dance was over he did not move away but waited for the next dance, which he seemed to assume was what I wanted, and indeed it was because he was good-looking, charming and flattering. The next number was slow and dreamy, but as I felt his arms tenderly wrap themselves around me I had the unholy thought that perhaps this was the octopus. I was soon distracted, however, by another problem as the strong elastic with which I had reinforced my panties began to cut into me like a strand of wire. When the music stopped I excused myself hurriedly and headed for the cloakroom. My friend Ann followed me to know what was happening. I explained about my panties.

"Take them off," she said, "and put them into the pocket of your coat."

"I can't go back out there with no panties on!" I gasped in horror.

"You've three choices," she declared, "go home, suffer on, or take them off."

"Put like that there seems to be no choice," I said, "but old Tom would say that it wasn't dacent."

The two of us were still laughing when one of my sisters came in to check up on how things were going for us and to issue half-time instructions. She soon solved the problem of the tight elastic with a nail-scissors and a safety-pin.

"Now," she instructed, "keep away from that blond guy."

"Why?" I asked, disappointed.

"He's a real Duffy's Circus operator: different venue every night."

"There had to be a catch," I said regretfully.

"Just make sure that you are not his catch for to-night," she warned, adding, "Keep away from the back of the hall now as all the old reserves are in from the pub and you'll be like a red rag to a bull to them."

My friend and I thought this very funny; nevertheless, when we went back into the hall we headed up to the area near the stage from which the band, who were also local, had a bird's eye view of the whole scene. One of them bent down to us to enquire, "Are ye steering clear of the old reserves?"

My handsome blond was back for the next dance and I wondered to myself how I was to shake off someone I really did not want to shake off. Ann had advised ignoring older sisters but I knew that home would be a very uncomfortable place if I did that and a curfew might even be imposed. So I lost myself in the crowd and the problem solved itself as school-pals gathered around and the rest of the night sped by. My handsome admirer soon replaced me with a blonde nearer his own age who was the proud possessor of a plunging neckline, which further convinced me of the desirability of a cleavage.

When the dance was over we spilled out onto the street, glad of the cool night air. At the end of the town we waited for the crowd from our road to gather together. Some were later than others coming back as they had gone walking with fellows or girls they had met at the dance, but all the first-nighters were present.

We all walked home singing and laughing and never noticed the length of our journey. When we arrived we found that my mother had left the fire stacked up to boil the kettle; we made tea quietly and went back over the events of the night in loud whispers. Then someone got the notion to fry rashers and sausages and while we waited for the fry to be ready we threshed out the night, sometimes going into fits of suppressed laughter when we recalled some incident. Finally we dragged ourselves upstairs and, after clearing paths to our beds, fell in, exhausted.

It was midday when the warm sun pouring in the window woke me the next day. My head was slightly muzzy from the throbbing sound of the band and the smoky atmosphere in the hall. Other heads were in worse condition to judge by the groaning and complaining that accompanied their getting up, while toes and shin-bones were examined for signs of wear and tear. A subdued crew, we all traipsed downstairs where my father had just arrived home from the creamery; he viewed us with an unsympathetic eye and announced in verse:

"There is no time for joy or laughter
In the cold grey dawn of the morning after."

This unwelcome shower of wisdom he followed with even more unwelcome instructions to get moving because the hay in the meadows by the river was ready for saving.

Making hay on a hot summer's day after a night spent dancing is not the easiest job in the world and we were a reluctant *meitheal*, but as the day wore on our youthful exuberance came to the surface and while we worked we discussed and relived yet again the momentous events of the previous night.

Little Bits
Of Darning

PETER WAS BORN with a romantic heart, filled with the love of music, song and women, and as his life went on it was the women who came to occupy the greatest share. He loved all women; his life and thoughts revolved around them: women he should have married, women he could have married, women he might have married, and even women he considered himself lucky not to have married. They were a constant source of entertainment to Peter and he was a constant source of entertainment to them.

Although he was of our parents' generation, that placed no barrier between Peter and young people. He could go to the pub with my father for a pint after Mass and yet come dancing with us that night, and he would be equally at home in both situations. He was a beautiful dancer and would glide the most awkward beginner around the dance-floor, making her feel as if all the dancing skill were hers. If a night was not going according to plan we would ask Peter to dance and he could be relied upon to help out at awkward moments. He even came dancing armed with a book to fill in the duller intervals.

Peter's origins were shrouded in romantic mystery: the way he put it himself was that he was the result of "a little bit of darning". He explained further that most families had a skeleton in the cupboard as a consequence of some member having deviated from the straight and narrow, and most families coped with these upsets and drew both erring one and consequence back into the fold. Peter termed the process of recovery from these upheavals as "little bits of darning". His own parents had had no children when his father had come home one night from a horse fair with a bouncing baby under his arm which he had presented to his wife. My mother expressed her doubts about this story but Peter swore that it was true and, true or otherwise, we found it intriguing.

He would describe his first experience of falling in love in great detail. Just sixteen, he had fallen head over heels for the daughter of a family down the road. So besotted was he that he sat all day on a stone wall opposite her house waiting to catch a glimpse of her. Finally her mother came out.

"Tell me, Peter," she enquired, "is it your first time?"

"Yes, mam," he answered respectfully and added, "It's killing me."

"Well now, Peter," she told him, "I'll give you a cure."

"Will you?" he asked eagerly.

"Yes indeed, Peter," she said consolingly. "Go home now like a good boy and take a fine dose of salts."

Peter would laugh heartily when telling this story and add, "Wasn't she a sound woman?"

He lived on a small farm, but didn't put much work into it, and when he got a legacy from America the first thing he did was to buy a piano. He had no idea how to play it so, to give himself time to learn, he rented out the farm. It being the first piano to come to our district, we all called to see Peter's unusual investment: it was a beauty with two brass candle-holders and every night he lit his candles and practised his playing. Sometimes, to take a rest from his piano practice, he picked up his fiddle, which he had played all his life as his father had taught him when he had been only a child, and while he played he danced around the house in total enjoyment of the music.

When he had mastered the piano he invited us all to a performance and we proved an appreciative if not very discerning audience. He also sang songs he had written himself and put music to and he recited verses he had composed about various local happenings. Any evening in Peter's house was great fun. It was also a house for card games and players came there from miles around. However, on some nights that were meant for card playing, Peter would not be in the right mood and so would turn them into musical nights instead, much to the annoyance of the cards enthusiasts. But Peter's violin poured forth music so sweet that the card players soon forgot their annoyance and danced off the floor with gusto.

Young and not-so-young lined up for half-sets and old men crippled with "the pains" found new pep in their step and bounced on the floor like garsoons. On other nights a concert would evolve and then we were all expected to do our party pieces. Ability had little to do with performance and if you could not dance you had to sing or recite; if you foundered in mid-verse everybody else came to the rescue and joined in. Card playing, on the other hand, was a serious business which often led to frayed tempers and arguments, but when these occurred Peter was always quick to clear the house.

Sometimes he would get a notion and write to all his old girlfriends with extravagant declarations of love that he did not mean and they, from previous experience of him, were smart enough not to take seriously. Letters he received in answer to his bold assertions he would read out for the entertainment of Bill, who was a great friend of his. After reading out a sentence that pleased him particularly he would say to Bill, "I will read that last sentence again for you so that you can feel the love expounding there". In his own letters, one of his more dramatic conclusions was, "If my pen were a pistol I'd blow out my brains for love of you," and on one occasion this protestation blew up in his face.

Former girlfriends who were safely married posed no threat to his romantic meanderings, but when one wrote from America that she was now a widow and was coming home to claim him for her own, Peter was thrown into a complete panic. He calmed down after a while and trotted off to Bill to ask for help in solving his desperate problem, but Bill had read too many "pen and pistol" letters to this same lady to have much sympathy with him, so he told Peter that the time had come to turn his pen into a pistol and blow his brains out, or else marry her.

Peter declared that he was caught on the horns of a dilemma and did not know which way to jump. In one way he was apprehensive at the prospect of her arrival, but in another way he was fascinated by the thought of meeting her again, and he mused about how things might develop. And when he had recovered from the initial shock he appeared to become quite philosophical about the whole affair.

It did seem to set him back a bit when he discovered that the gentle, soft-spoken slip of a girl with long blonde hair who had lived in his memory for twenty years had turned into a busty matron with brassy hair and a strident voice. But he recovered his composure and soon seemed to be enjoying escorting around his colourful Yank, as he called her. She was flamboyant and good humoured, which was very important to Peter who had said that there was only one eventuality which he could not overcome and that was if she had grown dull and boring. So Peter sang for us all:

"And when you think you're past love
It's then you find your last love
And you'll love her
As you never loved before."

Now that Peter was happy with his lot we relaxed a little, but at the same time we felt that there was no guarantee that he would see the whole thing through.

When the shock came it came not from Peter but from the Yank. One day she packed her bags and told Peter that although he had not changed, she had, and somehow she just could not visualize herself living in the depths of rural Ireland.

We thought that Peter would be devastated, but not a bit of it. So immediate was his recovery that Bill concluded he must have pulled a stroke: the Yank had gone away thinking that she had changed her mind, but Bill was sure that Peter had changed it for her. Whatever the truth of the matter, Peter was smiling, and when we questioned him about it he would only say that fate had destined him to keep many women happy rather than make one woman miserable.

Faigh Do Cóta

THE DANCES HELD on St Stephen's night, on Easter Sunday and at the summer carnival were gala occasions for me, not least because it was only during the holidays that I was allowed to go out dancing. Music was always provided by a local band whose members we all knew and whose repertoire was well tried and truly tested. So established were their routines that anyone who had been going to dances for a while could almost tell the time of night by the tune being played, and always before they played the national anthem they gave advance warning by playing "When The Saints Go Marching In". Anyone wanting to acquire a companion to walk her home needed to have sorted herself out by the time "The Saints" started up.

A couple who were seen dancing together for more than two dances was considered to be entering into serious negotiations, and if they went together for a drink at the mineral bar it was then considered that negotiations had been completed. There was plenty of flirting and fun between us and we girls joked amongst ourselves about different male approaches, which varied from "Can I see you home?" to "Would you like an orange?" or "Would you get your coat?", which last we termed a "Faigh do cóta" operation.

Reluctant to leave the secure ground of platonic friendship for the quicksand of romantic encounters, I walked myself home for many months, much to the annoyance of my best friend Ann, who declared that if I did my Leaving Cert without having been kissed my education would not be complete. She brought great pressure to bear and, after having failed to persuade me for some time, she decided finally that on St Stephen's night of my last year at school I was to be introduced into the kissing world, under any circumstances.

In the course of that night I met a young lad who was also doing his Leaving Cert but was away at boarding-school during term time. He was good fun and interesting, though he did not set my hair on fire, which the more experienced Ann had assured me was not necessary, though I had my doubts. After the dance we walked out along the road to the house where I was staying with friends. As we walked we chatted and it struck me that I would be feeling much more relaxed were it not for the prospect of the kissing which I expected was going to be part of the proceedings.

"Do you know something?" I said to him, "I've never been kissed before and I'm not so sure that I'm going to like it."

He stopped dead in his tracks and stared at me with such a shocked look on his face that I started laughing, and when he had recovered he joined in.

"God," he said, "you believe in the direct approach!"

"Well, it avoids complications," I said, "and I've got to start somewhere."

"Do you think we should start practising?" he asked, still laughing.

"Well, if we do, we'll wait until we get out under those trees further on," I said, because I was definitely not going to start practising right there in front of Mrs Lane's house. A sufferer from insomnia, Mrs Lane was forever telling my mother about the hours she spent looking out of the window at night and how long and boring it was. I had no intention of shortening the night for her.

When we arrived beneath the trees he put his arm around me and, looking over his shoulder, I could see the moon through the trees. I wondered would the moon still be in the same place after my first kiss and would I still be the same person. It was a strange, mildly exciting experience but his nose was cold, which put a slight damper on the proceedings. The moon did not dance in the sky nor the earth shake beneath my feet, and I told my companion that while it was OK I felt that kissing was a bit overrated. He assured me laughingly that it could improve with repetition, but it was a bad night for practising as a freezing grey frost covered the countryside, so we soon parted company.

The following week he went back to school and shortly afterwards I received from him a letter telling me that we would have to get together again at Easter to put in more practice. It had been his first kiss as well. He had not told me at the time, he wrote, because he had not wanted to undermine my confidence in his ability.

"You Can't Beat The Nuns"

IN MY MOTHER'S book the nuns were without
equal when it came to making a thorough job of anything. So she insisted that all her daughters spend
time with them in a domestic-science school to learn the
basic skills for survival and the social graces that the
nuns alone could impart; to prepare us for life, as she
put it. I protested vigorously, as the last thing I wanted
was to spend a year locked up with nuns. My mother,
however, reckoned that if my older sisters had needed
house-training I, because I was the youngest and most
useless, was in even greater need of it. My protests went
unheard; on occasions such as this when conflicting
opinions clashed my mother always won: she became
deaf and dumb and totally unmovable, and all arguments simply ground to a halt. A side of her that was
seldom seen, this steely determination came to the
surface when she deemed it necessary for the common
good; if something was right then no amount of arguing
would make it wrong, and vice versa, end of story.

So one September day I found myself in my late teens
heading reluctantly towards Drishane Convent, some
fifteen miles back the road from our home. In every
brood ability may be unevenly distributed, and when
domestic skills were allocated I was under the hen's
wing. On my very first day in Drishane I blotted my
copybook by telling the domestic-science teacher, Sister

162

Benignus – or Benny as she was generally known to her respectful pupils – that rice pudding should be flavoured with pepper. She raised her eyes to heaven and announced in regretful tones, "You do not appear to take after your sister Clare". And from then on for the entire year I was to live in the shadow of my more accomplished sister.

The head nun was a chubby, chirpy, correct little person with sparkling brown eyes and a wobbling chin. She always reminded me of a sprightly robin, and this birdlike appearance was emphasized by the Drishane coif which was peaked at the front. She was a stickler for correct behaviour and demanded that we all walk tall, and when she entered the dining-room she went around poking us between the shoulder-blades and saying in her chirpy voice, "Deportment, girls, deportment: always sit up straight and do not slouch". She believed in decorum in all things, and in law and order, and she ran her school on the well-oiled wheels of good planning and orderly routine. Her twenty-eight pupils were divided into four groups and rotated between cookery, sewing, housecraft and poultry; she made it clear that in each aspect this was to be a year of self-improvement for each of us, in which everything, no matter how trivial, was to be done well.

We were awakened at 7.30 every morning by Sister Ita clapping her hands along the dormitory where we slept in curtained cubicles; then she chanted "Benedicamus Domino", to which we were all supposed to answer "Deo Gratias" and jump out of bed. That was the theory; the reality, however, was that most of us groaned and complained and did not feel in the least like offering thanks. I would hang in there as long as I possibly could, but Sister Ita kept on going up and down until she had us all dug out of our beds. Beside each bed was a little dressing-table with an earthenware basin

and a jug of cold water, with the aid of which we washed
ourselves – upper half first from top down; then lower
half from bottom up.

We clattered along the polished wooden corridors
and down the wide stairs – using a different side each
week to balance the wear – and out into the grey dawn.
On winter mornings the old castle which stood beside
the path through the garden glistened with frost, while
light poured out through the stained-glass windows of
the little chapel. If any wisps of sleep still lingered in our
brains the sharp air of early morning soon cleared them
away, and by the time we had climbed the timber spiral
stairs to the chapel our minds were as alert and recep-
tive as they would ever be. With the coming of spring
this early morning walk was a lovely introduction to the
day as the mist rose from the lake beyond the lawn that
sloped away on the left-hand side of the path and the
dew sparkled on the overhanging trees which surrounded the lake.

Some of the grounds around Drishane were land-
scaped but saved from monotony by the old castle and
the hidden corners around the grey, stone buildings.
The gardens and lawns extended to the playing pitches
and the quiet fields of the convent farm stretched as far
as the eye could see. It was a gracious, restful place and
I passed a varied and interesting year there in blessedly
tranquil surroundings. We were taught all aspects of
cookery, household management and needlework; and
although not naturally endowed with domestic skills, I
learned that with good planning and organization the
tedium of housework could be reduced to a minimum.

In the laundry the ironing of linen table-cloths and
serviettes was carried out according to a set ritual.
When it came to instructions on how to iron a man's
shirt I expressed strenuous reservations but Sister Ita
simply swept them aside. The laundry itself was a large,

flag-stoned room with big earthenware sinks set against
the walls all around, and there was a huge old iron pull-
out clothes dryer for use in the winter months. The
windows of the laundry looked out over the orchard
where in summer the clothes fluttered on the line
between the apple-trees.

While one group was busy in the laundry another
prepared lunch in the kitchen, a big airy room with a
red, quarry-tiled floor and tall windows which looked
out over the sweeping driveway, playing pitches and
farm fields. It was dominated by a huge Aga cooker. It
was my first experience with an Aga and I decided that
if in later years I should ever be confined to a kitchen an
Aga would be my working companion. It was big, roomy,
comfortable and tolerant, almost like a caring grandmother sitting in the corner. It had a big boiling ring
that could carry many pots and a simmering ring of the
same size, together with hot ovens and gentle warming
ones.

Off the kitchen was a long pantry with a wire-mesh
window and long, timber, glass-fronted presses. On a
table under the window we made butter-rolls for the
afternoon tea. If the cooking group were efficient we ate
well and if not we suffered the consequences; as our own
critics we were pretty effective. The test of a good cook,
Sister Benignus told us, was to be able to recover from
a kitchen disaster and present the meal at the dining-
room table as a triumph. This was easier said than done
and we ate a few kitchen disasters which were very
recognizable as such, but as the year went on they
became fewer and fewer.

"Up-house" the group learned all about waxing and
polishing and were responsible for keeping the place
spick and span. We made our own polish – two cups of
turpentine and boiled oil and one cup of methylated
spirits and vinegar – which fed as well as polished the

furniture. Amongst the other skills we acquired were how to pack a case efficiently and how to serve a meal to a VIP guest. And in all their teaching of us the nuns were pleasant and good-humoured, while letting us know that when in Rome you did as the Romans did.

Elsewhere in a much larger part of the school other pupils, in for a five-year stretch, were preoccupied with Inter and Leaving Certs, but we were blissfully free of exams. While others swotted we had an end-of-term concert and play, a humorous depiction of the lifestyle of the convent which the nuns laughed at as heartily as anyone. Having scripted and produced the entertainment, I was rewarded with a prize for my first exercise in the dramatic arts. Prizes were presented by the nun who was responsible for encouraging our spiritual and creative development; a very sensitive, holy nun, Sister Eithne possessed a quirky, wry sense of humour, and as my prize she ceremoniously presented me with a facecloth and a box of soap.

With me in Drishane was Ann who had been a fellow student at the old school across the fields and later at the secondary school in town. One evening before going to the chapel for night prayers she decided to pin her long hair in coils on the top of her head. She had not foreseen how peculiar it would look when her school beret was perched on top; but the operation had taken longer than anticipated and there was no time to take her hair down as we were late already. We ran breathlessly down the path and up the long, spiral stairs to the chapel. As we ran I got a fit of laughing every time I looked at the creation on the top of her head, and then we scurried at last into our seats just as the Reverend Mother started the rosary. Kneeling beside Ann I tried hard to suppress the urge to giggle, but while I had some success the girls in the seats behind had none. Gasps of suppressed laughter burst from the rows of girls behind us and those in front, when they heard the noise, looked back and beheld the amazing hairstyle with the beret perched so precariously on top, and then they started shaking with amusement. Nothing induces laughter as much as the knowledge that one should not, especially when everyone else is trying to stop laughing as well. Even the sobering thought that behind us were rows of demurely praying nuns did nothing to control the situation. It was a great relief when night prayers ended and we could escape from the church but first we had to walk down the aisle past rows of serene-faced nuns. As I passed the final row I shot a quick glance at the head nun; she caught my eye and gave a knowing smile, and the incident was never mentioned afterwards.

Young novices entered the Drishane order in October and March and watching these black-garbed figures in the chapel I was impressed by their courage. Of course, some found that the religious life was not for them and left, but amongst those who stayed the one who impressed me most of all was Sister Gemma. A pretty girl, bubbling with good humour and gaiety, she seemed even as she walked to bounce off the ground with her veil flying and her long black dress swirling, almost as if earth had no claim on her. Some years later, while she was still quite young, she died of cancer, but at her funeral I felt no sadness, sure that she had gone to where all her thoughts and motivations had had their origin.

My year spent at the convent gave me my first experience of nuns and I observed their lifestyle with fascination. In many ways I found it intriguing and attractive though I was shocked by their lack of personal freedom. The fact that so many women lived together under one roof in apparent harmony impressed me as a tribute to their self-discipline and tolerance, and although there must inevitably have been moments of friction between them we never witnessed them. United in religious zeal, their community was cemented together by their love of God and their interest in their pupils. The School of Housecraft there has been closed for many years now, but although I had argued with my mother that a year spent there would be a year wasted, I have always been glad since then that she got the better of me in that argument.

Back Across
The Fields

DANNY LOOKED AT the world through eyes that saw the beauties of the countryside which we usually ran past as we played. Because he was less robust than other children he walked more slowly, and often he called us back to look at what he had discovered. Ours was a mixed school in which girls and boys treated each other as equals, and if a row broke out we girls kicked shins and pulled hair to assert ourselves. In the classroom the boys stuck our long hair into ink-wells and used the nibs of pens to inject their venom into our bare necks and elbows whenever the opportunity arose. But while Danny played football with the boys at lunch-time he never took part in the ink-dipping and nib-prodding skulduggery that the others engaged in. Those who sat in front of him had no need to fear attack from the rear, for Danny was too gentle to inflict hardship on anyone.

It was he who introduced me to my first telephone. It was a stone. In the morning if he had passed to school ahead of me he placed a stone on top of the old bridge. Soon the children of each family had their own stone and on arrival at the bridge in the morning we could see by the stones who had gone before us; if it was early and we had time to spare we might sit on the bridge and wait for the others.

Our schoolbags, made from a strong, green material,

we called "purses" and they needed to be strong for they were battered, bruised and dirtied through encounters with hedges and muddy gaps. Some had two armbands through which we looped our hands so that they could hang off our backs. Danny's, however, hung off a long strap that swung around his neck and knocked off his boney knees. He always had more in his bag than the rest of us because he never tidied it out but simply carried his books forward from year to year.

The hands of all the children going to our school were brown and mostly muddy; all, that is, except Danny's, which were pale and blue-veined with long, tapering, sensitive fingers. And on these fingers pet birds perched, quite unafraid, when he stretched out his delicate hands to them. The rest of us stood back and watched him do this because if we moved close the frightened birds flew away. His relationship with the birds placed Danny a cut above the rest of us in my book, but he never thought himself superior on this account and he was simply surprised that we could not also do what came to him so naturally.

He spent much of the day looking up at the sky and watching the clouds, and he had names for the different cloud formations. Sometimes on a summer evening he persuaded us all to lie down on the grass and look up at the sky with him, and when we did this we became aware, ironically, of the world at our feet. Here in the grass were ladybirds, grasshoppers and ants, which we called pismires, and all the teeming insect life that we normally walked over unseeing. My sister Clare pulled the long blades of grass and persuaded us that she could play music through them, and sometimes she succeeded though her audience was not always entirely appreciative. We pulled the long-stemmed dandelions and blew away their soft, fluffy hats to tell the time: one o'clock, two o'clock – each puff an hour. Not as accurate as Greenwich Mean Time but more enjoyable. If a tall foxglove with its cascading purple flowers happened to be growing near us, we went through a routine of cracking the bells, or "fairy thimbles" as we called them, making sure first that there were no wasps visiting inside. We also used some unfortunate flowers – usually marguerites or other large daisies – for games of "he loves me, he loves me not".

Danny conveyed to us some of his awareness and appreciation of life. Looking at life from soft, brown, moist eyes, he saw more than the rest of us and coaxed us to see it too. When he put his mind to his studies, he was the star pupil, but learning enjoyed no great priority in his life and some mornings he arrived in school with his sack unopened since leaving the previous evening. If the master was suspected to be on a rampage Danny would sit on a stone in the last field before the school and run off his exercise or lessons. He had a nose that dried up in the summer like the hill streams, but in winter the sleeve of his jumper was in constant use as an emergency handkerchief. Tissues, of course, were unheard of and the torn-up sheets that we were supposed to use as hankies often wound up being used as sails for boats in the *glaise* or for other more necessary pursuits.

Danny's hair had a mind of its own and stuck out in all directions. His mother used laughingly to say that a scrubbing brush was necessary to subdue it every morning, but before long it would again resemble a furze bush.

After leaving school he remained on the home farm and when his parents died he lived a contented bachelor existence on his own. Many years later, on a cold January day when the ground was covered with snow, I called to his house; he was not at home but I finally ran him to earth in a neighbour's field where he stood surrounded by neighbouring children. The years had brought touches of premature grey to his wayward hair but his brown eyes held the same trusting, merry look. As we walked together down towards his house I told him that I intended walking back across the fields to the old school and asked him to come with me. I could see that he felt that the journey might be too much for him but as always his spirit was willing, so we set out to retrace our footsteps for the first time since we had gone to school together.

The paths were now overgrown and the hedges had closed in over the stepping stones that spanned the ditches, but we burrowed our way through as snow tumbled down on top of us from high branches. At the old school we found that the trees had grown in around it and grass had grown up to the window-sills; it stood huddled in the arms of nature which now claimed it for its own as ivy trailed across its gaping windows. Where once children had laughed and shouted, now the cawing of crows from the tree-tops was the only sound. There was about it a peacefulness, as if the years of learning had blended into the walls and the grey stones were now sheltered by the overhanging branches.

We went around the back to inspect the old dry toilets: now they were crumbling with age and we laughed as we recalled the request of "Bhfuil cead agam dul amach". Leaning over the rusty gate beside the school we looked back across the valley and Danny looked up at the sky and started to talk about the clouds and it was as if time had stood still.

When we arrived back at Danny's thatched cottage the snow had started to come down again and we were glad to poke up the fire and make the tea. As I sat beside the fire I looked around his large kitchen, which bore all the signs of the freedom of bachelor living; no "fussy woman" disturbed the leisurely pace of Danny's life. He had plans for a new house and he spread them out on the table and we studied them. It would have amenities that this old one lacked, including central heating, but I wondered if Danny might find it difficult to leave his old house. He took me into a room off the kitchen to show me a magnificent oil painting and a large mahogany sideboard that would have been a collector's dream. We talked about his love of birds and I promised to paint a picture of pheasants for his new house.

As I walked out the long yard I turned to wave to Danny, who was framed in the doorway of his long, low, thatched house. With the snow on the thatch and the light from the deep-set window cutting into the darkness, it was like a scene from a Christmas card. I walked home across the fields, memories churning around in my mind. The moon had risen high in the sky and the snow-covered countryside stretched out around me, while the frosty grass crunched beneath my feet. When I saw the lights of our own house I slowed my footsteps, reluctant to leave behind this outdoor calmness that enfolded me.

During the summer that followed I painted the picture for Danny's new house, but it was destined never to hang there. One day in early autumn a phone call came to say that he had died, quietly, just as he had lived. At his funeral I met many of our old school friends and we shared a feeling of vulnerability brought about by the fact that he was the first of our class to go. Some of them I had not met since leaving the old schoolhouse in the fields, so on an occasion which combined both happiness and sadness there was much reminiscing. And as I drove back past his silent house that night I stopped and got out to lean on his rusty gate, and I felt glad that he had never left his old home that was somehow where he belonged, and where his spirit would always be at peace.

To School Through The Fields

"It is a book which has taken us down a delightful boreen into a world that is now largely gone, but which so many of us can remember with so much affection." *Cork Examiner*

"This is the story of ordinary people and ordinary occurrences. But they were a fine people and there was a gentle nobility about the occurrences which shaped their lives." *Irish Post*

"Her reflection of a quality of life with which real people everywhere can identify marks out her book as a masterpiece." *The Corkman*

"My advice to the visitor: if you only buy one book on this trip, then let it be this one." *Cara*

"Beautiful and gentle. . . full of character and characters." *Yorkshire Post*

"She reminds us of that time when the only fertiliser that was spread on the earth came out of the rear ends of animals and it was still possible for human beings to swim in the rivers and call on one another without invitation." *The Mail on Sunday*

"Lyrical reminiscences of growing up Irish, recounted with both wistfulness and wit. . . these stories evoke a time when family life consisted of a procession of joyful celebrations, when neighbors tended to one another's needs as a matter of course, and when nature was a benevolent presence, intimately connected with every soul." *Kirkus Review*

"A delightful evocation of Irishness and of the author's deep-rooted love of "the very fields of home", this picture of bucolic life in an earlier time, with its rituals of religion and the antics of local characters, has universal appeal." *Publishers Weekly*

Paperback £4.95

Close to the Earth: Poems of Country Life

"A charming collection of poems of country life. . . accompanied by the very distinctive drawings of Brian Lalor."
Evening Press
"What's refreshing about her verse is its simplicity; not for Taylor the impenetrable musings that seem to be so fashionable these days. Odes on Nature and Those Were The Days themes predominate but she has the confidence to tackle weightier topics. . . Taylor has a marvellous gift for painting a complete word picture in just 8 to 20 short lines and she can be cutting too." *Phoenix*

Paperback £4.95

An Evening With Alice Taylor

"You've read the book, the diary and the poems, now hear a selection of them all and the voice of the author on tape in *An Evening With Alice Taylor*. The 90-minute tapes is full of fond memories and thoughts of childhood and country life."
Southern Star

C-90 cassette tape £4.95 (inc VAT)

An Irish Country Diary

"This delightful lady has done it again. Here is a diary with a difference. It is divided into the 12 months of the year, each month preceded by a piece of home-spun wisdom. The centre of the book has reproductions of some of the beautiful paintings by Mildred Anne Butler, with a short biography of this almost forgotten artist. The pages are blank and the dates are left for the owner to fill in herself. A really lovely book." *Women's Club Magazine*

"Superbly illustrated from paintings by Mildred Anne Butler. . . would make an excellent gift." *Southern Star*

"For each month of the year the importance of weather and growth of farm and animal are followed, with the coming of February and the first daffodils and primroses, and so through the lengthening days of early summer and autumn. A lovely book." *Electrical Mail*

Hardback £9.95 (inc VAT)